THE Daredevil Book for Dogs

What Dogs Really Think!

NICK GRIFFITHS

ILLUSTRATED BY DAVID MOSTYN

ARCTURUS

Nick Griffiths is an author and journalist because NASA wouldn't let him be an astronaut. He has written *Dalek I Loved You: A Memoir* and *Who Goes There*, both based around Doctor Who, and the comic novel *In the Footsteps of Harrison Dextrose*, while writing largely for *Radio Times*. He owns a cat named Columbo, who has failed to solve any murder cases, and would love to own a dog but can't get past the idea of picking up its poo in a small plastic bag.

Illustrator **David Mostyn** began his career as a commercial artist in advertising, then moved into publishing and set up his own company Mostyn Partners in 1977. David has worked for 30 years in comic strips, producing drawings for DC Thomson, Marvel Comics and DC Comics, among others. He is married with two children and one cat, and lives in Oxford.

ARCTURUS

This edition published in 2009
by Arcturus Publishing Limited
26/27 Bickels Yard,
151–153 Bermondsey Street,
London SE1 3HA

ISBN: 978-1-84837-207-8
AD000142EN

Printed in China

Contents

Introduction

Hello, my name is Jason. Yes, it is an odd name for a dog, but then not many dogs are named after Jason Orange out of Take That, on whom the lady of the house had developed an unsettling crush.

Otherwise, my human companions – who prefer to think of themselves as 'owners' – are not terribly original. Both greying of hair, they paint their walls magnolia, consider the turnip to be a sophisticated vegetable and have a toilet rota (she always first, since he has a propensity to 'wilt the wallflowers', as they euphemistically put it). They are not what you would call adventurous.

Do I complain? Do I nudge them with a damp nose, suggesting an end to their inertia? No, I do not. For a couple of very good reasons:

🐾 I am old now, 98 in dog years, and inertia suits me fine (calls of nature notwithstanding).

🐾 I am also a dog. Dogs don't rock the boat. It's simply not in our nature. We are loyal, dependable, subservient – their rock. We like it that way; it's so embedded in our DNA that to shift it would take a JCB the size of Alaska and a driver more stubborn than a red-wine stain on Snow White's sleeve.

What have I achieved during my 98 dog years? Plenty and nothing (should you consider sleeping an awful lot to be 'nothing'). Oh, I've had my moments.

> 1. There have been romances, I can't deny. Actually, there have been 57 of them, not that I'm counting. That's 57 pups who call me 'Pa' (or would, if they ever saw me) – 57 varieties of Yours Truly, which is why some of the more cynical bitches in the neighbourhood have taken to calling me 'Heinz' and steering a wide berth. They needn't worry, I'm too old for all those shenanigans now. More's the pity.

> **2.** I once saved a child from drowning! Well, sort of. It was more by luck than judgement, really. I'd been paddling in the sea, became tired and as I was lazily being washed back to shore a passing child clung to my fur. I don't even think it was in any trouble, but no one saw it that way and I was proclaimed a hero. I'm not about to explain it to them. Not that I could, unless someone finds a dog whisperer who can translate 'Woof! Woof! Woof!' into 'Actually, the kid just held on to me as I floated home.'

So this book is my attempt to pass on my plentiful knowledge. It's a 'compendium of wisdom', if you will, both practical and insightful – the relationship between a dog and its human companions deconstructed. I'll tell you how to attract their attention, how to beat them at Tug of War, how to steal their food – much tastier than ours – off their plates, how to petrify the ones who deliver the mail, even if you're a small dog with a pitiful yap, and why, precisely, we are their 'best friend'.

It's all a game of psychology, I have realized. Let them think they're in charge, but do your own thing and take the praise/grub. They call it 'loyalty', I call it 'necessity'. Plus, I'll be telling you how to make anything from your own luxury kennel to a space rocket, explaining how Laika got famous, why Lassie was a right swot and revealing the truth behind the legend of the White Doggy-Do.

I make no bones about this (if you'll excuse the pun): every dog should read this book. We could all do with a little more self-belief, we could all take more control of our lives, we could all become more in touch with our inner dolphin (see page 8, if you're confused).

Just think: a new dog obedience class opens every day somewhere in the world. Talk about being taken for mugs! It doesn't have to be that way. *The Daredevil Book*

for Dogs will teach you to rise up (if you're not feeling too drowsy), to throw off your shackles of oppression (provided they land in a neat pile) and to say a firm 'No!' to your human companions (followed swiftly by a meeker 'Yes', then a hasty 'Sorry about that').

You are a Dog and that is a Noble Thing To Be.

Origin of the Species

Do you know where we dogs are descended from? Thought not. Luckily for you, I do and I have brought my theory along to prove it.

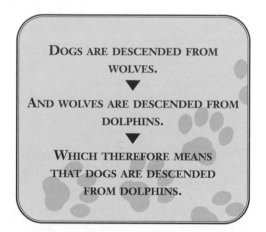

DOGS ARE DESCENDED FROM WOLVES.

▼

AND WOLVES ARE DESCENDED FROM DOLPHINS.

▼

WHICH THEREFORE MEANS THAT DOGS ARE DESCENDED FROM DOLPHINS.

How can this possibly be true? Let's forget all about wolves and cut to the chase.

The most obvious link between dogs and dolphins is that we're both terribly intelligent. Dolphins invented wind farms and catalytic converters in cars. Dogs invented non-biological washing powders, Stephen Hawking and the board game *Risk*. I assume you see my point.

But how did it happen, this curious evolution from dolphin into dog? From gentle sea creature to land-based stud? I'll tell you…

Several million years ago, dolphins were swimming happily around in the oceans, occasionally jumping through hoops and being friendly to tuna. Back then dogs didn't exist. (Boo!) Obviously this was a disgraceful state of affairs which had to be corrected, so evolution took a hand.

One day, a dolphin jumped through a hoop and accidentally landed on dry land. He might have died there, had he not been spotted by an early human whose name was Mmph. Mmph had always wanted a dog, even though he wasn't sure what one was. So Mmph took the dolphin home, named him Rover and started treating him as if he were a dog: making him a nice kennel, playing games of Fetch, feeding him tins of dog food, that sort of thing.

And the dolphin began to believe that he was a dog! He began to live on the land – indeed, he would have drowned, had he gone back to his old dolphin ways. Instead, he started to dream of chasing cats and over a period of months, possibly longer, his fins fell off and he grew legs. His fur – dolphins are mammals, too, remember – grew shaggier and his head became much more attractive. In short, he upgraded and turned into a dog.

One night, when Mmph was well into old age – by which I mean that he was very old, not that he found pensioners fascinating – he was taking Rover for a walk when he bumped into Bleugh, who was also walking a dog! (Bleugh, too, had rescued a beached dolphin, which had evolved into a dog. A lady dog. You see where this is heading…)

And so Rover and Bleugh's dog, whose name was Fifi, had lots of puppies and that is how I am descended from dolphins!

Famous Dogs in History

1. Lassie

A simpering film-and-television hound, who became famous for being brown and white and for regularly rescuing humans from mortal danger, despite being just a dog. This holier-than-thou Collie first starred in *Lassie Come Home* in 1943 and was an instant hit (although, during the middle of a war, it's tempting to suggest that people will watch any old rubbish).

The plot ran like this: Lassie went away and then she came home again. Hurrah. Grown men and women wept. Hanky rations became scarce. Children wanted to own Lassie. The catchphrase of the day became, 'Here, girl!' The bitch who played Lassie made millions, sacked her owners and could be seen falling out of seedy nightclubs by night, a rich Doberman on each paw. She could do no wrong.

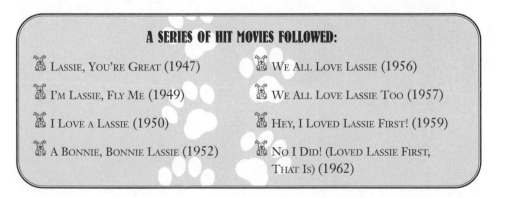

A SERIES OF HIT MOVIES FOLLOWED:

🐕 Lassie, You're Great (1947)

🐕 I'm Lassie, Fly Me (1949)

🐕 I Love a Lassie (1950)

🐕 A Bonnie, Bonnie Lassie (1952)

🐕 We All Love Lassie (1956)

🐕 We All Love Lassie Too (1957)

🐕 Hey, I Loved Lassie First! (1959)

🐕 No I Did! (Loved Lassie First, That Is) (1962)

But then: disaster. Lassie had spread herself too thin. The plot to *No I Did! (Loved Lassie First, That Is)* involved Lassie eating some dog food then falling asleep. The sleeping part, taking in only the occasional twitch, lasted for three days, four hours and 27 minutes. It was directed by Andy Warhol.

People got bored with the dependable Collie dog and her distinctive bark. Hey, it was the Swinging Sixties! Who wanted a dog trailing around after them during a period of Free Love?

AND SO THE SLIDE BEGAN:

🐾 Oh, Right, It's Lassie Again. Great (1966)

🐾 God, Please, Not Lassie (1968)

🐾 I Never Liked Lassie Anyway (1971)

🐾 I Hated Her First! (1972)

🐾 Lassie Does Dallas (1974)*

* Lassie was too drunk to perform several scenes in this movie and was replaced by a Dachshund named Steve, painted brown and white.

You might have thought that was the end of the Lassie franchise, but no. The nadir came with:

🐾 Lassie, You Mongrel (1976).

That movie, questioning Lassie's parentage, was the final straw. One night, the bitch who played Lassie was found face down in her own vomit outside the Ritzy nightclub. She had died of a 'Beef with Tender Rabbit Pieces in Mum's Rich Gravy' overdose.

Still, Lassie will never be forgotten. Which can't be helped.

Games Dogs Can Play

1. Fetch

The standard, the classic, the father of all doggie games. Fetch. Otherwise known by us old dogs as 'Oh No, Not Fetch Again'. Sure, retrievers like fetching things – the clue's in the name. But what about the rest of us? Does the Canary Dog like fetching things? Or the New Guinea Singing Dog? No! They like small yellow birds and karaoke, respectively.

Me, I loved fetching things as a puppy, but the novelty wore off over the years. Run to stick, tongue flapping like windsock. Pick up stick. Run back with stick. Drop stick. Run to stick, tongue flapping like windsock. Pick up stick … yadi-yadi-yadi-ya. Repeat ad infinitum.

You could die of boredom reading about it, let alone doing it! So here's a cunning plan I've devised if you want to get out of playing Fetch.

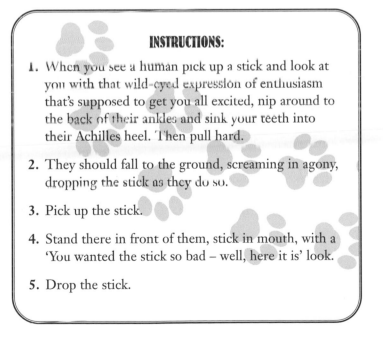

INSTRUCTIONS:

1. When you see a human pick up a stick and look at you with that wild-eyed expression of enthusiasm that's supposed to get you all excited, nip around to the back of their ankles and sink your teeth into their Achilles heel. Then pull hard.

2. They should fall to the ground, screaming in agony, dropping the stick as they do so.

3. Pick up the stick.

4. Stand there in front of them, stick in mouth, with a 'You wanted the stick so bad – well, here it is' look.

5. Drop the stick.

Doubt they'll try that one again. But if they do, simply repeat 1–5. An aversion process ironically named by humans after Pavlov's dog. Try a dose of your own, mister/missus!

1.1. Fetch from Water

This one's a killer. Kids especially love it. They do it to catch you unawares.

So they're waving the stick around and some dumb mutt's focusing on the wood alone, failing to check what's up ahead. A few false throws – curse you, human, just throw the stick! I'm desperate for stick. Gimme that lovely, yummy, chewy stick. And suddenly they let it loose. Off it flies, swirling through the air and the mutt's off like a bat out of hell, watching that stick as it arcs upwards and… Hey, what the hell's this?! It's… Brrrrrrrrrrrr… Hang on, I'm in water! I'm freezing! What is this?! It's only the sea! I've gone swimming by mistake!

Your fleas are panicking, building rafts from bits of flotsam, your head's in a whirl, your legs are paddling for all they're worth – and the human's back there on the bank, laughing. Not with you, but at you!

The ignominy. You're an idiot. You're a schmuck. You're the lowest of the low. Amoeba think you're a dummy.

Fear not, my sodden-furred friend, for I have a cunning plan for you too:

INSTRUCTIONS:

1. Sod the stick. Just keep swimming.

That's it! Easy! Their delighted, braying laughter will soon turn to silence, followed by anguished cries. They'll be pleading with you to come back!

If you're lucky, one or more of them may even dive in after you. Ignore them – just keep swimming. Eventually you'll reach Polynesia, or somewhere nice like that. Then they'll be sorry.

Things Famous Humans Said About Dogs, and What They Really Meant

'HEAVEN GOES BY FAVOUR. IF IT WENT BY MERIT, YOU WOULD STAY OUT
AND YOUR DOG WOULD GO IN' – MARK TWAIN, AUTHOR
Peter thinks your dog's great but that you don't cut the mustard.

'A HEART-BEAT, AT MY FEET' – EDITH WHARTON, AUTHOR
Yikes! My heart's fallen out!

'A DOG TEACHES A BOY FIDELITY, PERSEVERANCE, AND TO TURN AROUND THREE TIMES BEFORE LYING DOWN' – ROBERT BENCHLEY, AUTHOR

I used to play Ring-A-Ring-A-Roses with my dog.

'SOME OF MY BEST LEADING MEN HAVE BEEN DOGS AND HORSES' – ELIZABETH TAYLOR, ACTRESS

Don't talk to me about Richard Burton.

'A DOOR IS WHAT A DOG IS PERPETUALLY ON THE WRONG SIDE OF' – OGDEN NASH, WRITER

I'm not entirely sure what I'm on about.

'A DOG HAS THE SOUL OF A PHILOSOPHER' – PLATO, PHILOSOPHER

That dog just ate my soul.

'I'VE CAUGHT MORE ILLS FROM PEOPLE SNEEZING OVER ME AND GIVING ME VIRUS INFECTIONS THAN FROM KISSING DOGS' – BARBARA WOODHOUSE, DOG TRAINER

I'd steer well clear of me if I were you.

'IT IS FATAL TO LET ANY DOG KNOW THAT HE IS FUNNY, FOR HE IMMEDIATELY LOSES HIS HEAD AND STARTS HAMMING IT UP' – PG WODEHOUSE, AUTHOR

Never let a dog know he is funny, or his head will fall off.

'LOVE ME, LOVE MY DOG' – SAINT BERNARD OF CLAIRVAUX

Will you canonize my dog too, please?

'OUTSIDE OF A DOG, A BOOK IS MAN'S BEST FRIEND. INSIDE OF A DOG, IT'S TOO DARK TO READ' – GROUCHO MARX, COMEDIAN

Dogs are dark inside. (I know, it baffled me too. Is this guy trying to be funny?)

'ALL KNOWLEDGE, THE TOTALITY OF ALL QUESTIONS AND ALL ANSWERS, IS CONTAINED IN THE DOG' – FRANZ KAFKA, AUTHOR

That dog's just eaten my encyclopedia.

Things for Dogs to Build

1. The Kennel

Every dog's kennel is his castle. (Unless you get to sleep indoors in the snugly warm, in which case you will see a kennel for what it actually is: a small hut open to the elements, offering fewer creature comforts than a night spent among amorous porcupines. So for the purposes of this bit of the book, let's imagine you know no better than to consider a kennel to be the height of luxury, a padded pamper-dome where the days are idyllic and the nights slide past like velour crocodiles.)

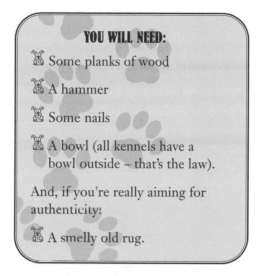

YOU WILL NEED:

- Some planks of wood
- A hammer
- Some nails
- A bowl (all kennels have a bowl outside – that's the law).

And, if you're really aiming for authenticity:

- A smelly old rug.

You might want to get a human to help you. Or you can be stubborn and end up with your tail nailed to your nose and a bowl trapped up your bottom. It's entirely up to you.

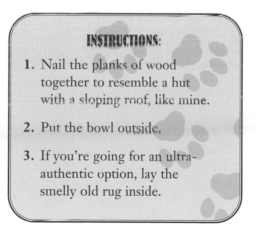

INSTRUCTIONS:

1. Nail the planks of wood together to resemble a hut with a sloping roof, like mine.

2. Put the bowl outside.

3. If you're going for an ultra-authentic option, lay the smelly old rug inside.

Hey presto! You're happy as Larry! (Provided that Larry is that mangy old Labrador who used to sleep down by the compost heap, under an awning made of tramps' trousers pinned together with fossilized Brontosaurus drool.)

The Great Escape

Human companions off on their holidays? So where does that leave you, my furry friend? Surplus to requirements and bang to rights at the local kennels, that's where. But you can avoid all that rowdy pining for home with only strangers for company if you pick one of the following cunning escape plans. (If you recognize any of them from popular war movies, that is purely coincidental.)

1. Three Tunnels

Dig three tunnels. Why three? Because if the German guards… sorry, the kennels staff discover one, you still have two left! And if they discover two, you still have one left! And if they discover all three – enjoy your stay!

How to do this without any kennels staff noticing? Simple. Knock up a pair of trousers that look like the illustration opposite and that exactly fit over your back legs. Secure them with a pair of braces.

Every time you dig, you don't want to be building up a pile of soil to one side – that's a dead giveaway. So hide it in your trouser legs! Then, when you're taken out for a walk, discreetly let the soil slip to the ground, where it won't be spotted. Lay a soil-coloured rug over any holes you've dug to disguise them.

When discussing your tunnels with other inmates… dogs, consider using codewords as 'Tunnels' might be a bit obvious. How about 'Tom', 'Dick' and 'Harry'? Purely off the top of my head.

When you're finished, make a break for it one night under cover of darkness. Suddenly, you're free! What you do then, I have no idea.

2. The Old 'He's Behind You!' Trick

This one's for inmates… I mean dogs, who share a cell… I mean a kennel. When one of the kennels staff opens the door to bring food, one of you hides behind the door with a big stick. The other stands in front of it, looking innocent. As the human steps into the kennel – 'Thwack!' from behind. They're out for the count. You then run like the wind!

Note: you might have problems holding the stick.

3. Make a Papier-mâché Model of Yourself

How to escape from Alcatraz... I mean the kennels, while still looking to nosey staff as if you are tucked up in bed? It may sound impossible, but it's not. You build a papier-mâché model of yourself and leave it in your bed on the night you escape, having previously tunnelled through a wall using a home-made pickaxe.

You can collect scraps of paper from around the place and steal glue and paints from the modelling club to make your model look lifelike. Then simply make your model while no one's looking (see results below).

Who's that with a paw up at the back? Yes? How do you make the home-made pickaxe? Use your ingenuity! I can't explain everything!

SPOT THE DIFFERENCE

4. The One-Final-Wish Confusion

When a dog gets very, very old or is very, very ill, sometimes humans have it 'put down'. Not in the 'You're rubbish!' sense, merely undermining your confidence, no. It's much worse than that: this is 'put down' as in 'given a lethal injection and put down in the ground. Six feet under. Nailed to one's kennel. Deceased.' A terrifying state of affairs. And you never know when it's coming.

One terrible day in July, a few years back, I was hauled into the car and driven I knew not where. My owners were strangely quiet; there was tension in the air: you could smell the guilt in everything they did.

I'd heard about this 'put down' business from the Schnauzer next door and began to fear the worst. 'So this is how it ends,' I thought, even though I felt perfectly all right and was only going on 27.

When the car stopped, I was looking around for a priest to perform the last rites... But it turned out it was only the kennels! I was so happy I'd have stayed there for a decade!

Later, I became convinced this had all been a psychological trick to make the kennels feel like the best of a bad job. But the explanation turned out to be a lot more straightforward. I discovered, once my human companions returned from their holiday, that all that silence and tension in the car, the slow ticking of the dashboard clock, had been because she'd just admitted to sleeping with his brother.

Dogs in Animation: A Handy Guide

For reasons of space, this list is by no means exhaustive, however it should get you by in the unlikely event that you're ever tested on it in school.

Deputy Dawg

WHO IS/WAS? The law-enforcement equivalent of someone who lives in a trailer.

PURPOSE IN LIFE: Buttering up the Sheriff, foiling Musky (a muskrat) and Vince (a gopher) who try to steal his food.

WELL, DID HE? What do you think? It's a cartoon. Where are the laughs if the Sheriff thinks Dawg's done a great job and Musky and Vince go hungry?

OBSCURE FACT: Musky was originally voiced by an actual muskrat, named Albert, who was owned by Rita Hayworth. When the show became a hit, Rita got jealous and asked for him back.

Dogtanian and the Three Muskehounds

WHO ARE/WERE? Canine cartoon versions of Alexandre Dumas's classic literary characters D'Artagnan and the Three Musketeers.

ARE YOU SERIOUS? I am.

THAT'S THE WORST PUN TITLE I'VE EVER HEARD! Tell me about it!

I MIGHT AS WELL PRODUCE A CARTOON TITLED *DOGALICE'S ADVENTURES IN WONDERHOUND*! I know!

PURPOSE IN LIFE: Serving the king of France back in the 17th century.

AND THEY'RE CARTOON DOGS? Right.

OBSCURE FACT: *Dogtanian and the Three Muskehounds* was rubbish.

Droopy

WHO IS/WAS? A dog who spoke slowly.

PURPOSE IN LIFE: To find everything a bit much.

IS THAT IT? I know, it's a bit much, isn't it?

OBSCURE FACT: Off-screen, Droopy was actually very happy. Sadly, playing such a dour character led him into depression and he took his own life in 1963.

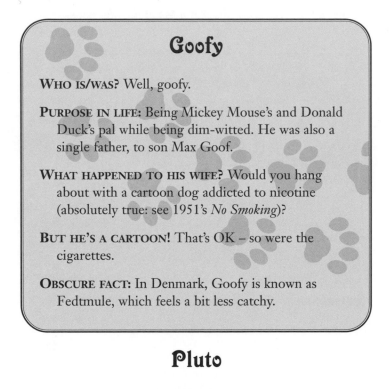

Goofy

WHO IS/WAS? Well, goofy.

PURPOSE IN LIFE: Being Mickey Mouse's and Donald Duck's pal while being dim-witted. He was also a single father, to son Max Goof.

WHAT HAPPENED TO HIS WIFE? Would you hang about with a cartoon dog addicted to nicotine (absolutely true: see 1951's *No Smoking*)?

BUT HE'S A CARTOON! That's OK – so were the cigarettes.

OBSCURE FACT: In Denmark, Goofy is known as Fedtmule, which feels a bit less catchy.

Pluto

WHO IS/WAS? Very much like Goofy.

PURPOSE IN LIFE: To be confused with Goofy.

OBSCURE FACT: He isn't Goofy.

Snoopy

WHO IS/WAS? Charlie Brown's Beagle.

PURPOSE IN LIFE: To outwit his master and to snooze on top of the roof of his kennel.

WAS IT A FLAT ROOF? No.

SLOPING ON EITHER SIDE? Yup.

ER... Leave it!

OBSCURE FACT: Cartoon Beagles find lying on the apex of a roof perfectly comfortable.

Scooby-Doo

WHO IS/WAS? A cowardly Great Dane, ghost-hunting member of Mystery Inc., comprising Fred, Daphne, Velma and Shaggy.

WHAT ABOUT SCR... Lalalala.

WHAT ABOU... Lalalalala.

BU... Blahblahblahblahblah.

SCRAP... Never. Ever. Ever. Mention the name of that tawdry, wimpy, soul-destroying World's Most Annoying Cartoon Character Ever.

WHO? SCRAPPY-DOO? Right, that's it. I'm leaving.

OBSCURE FACT: You'll have to fill that in yourself.

Dogs in Song

Since time immemorial – or 1956, at least – we have been the subject of man's musical noodlings. Sadly, much of it has been utter twaddle…

1956 – PERRY COMO – **HOT DIGGITY (DOG ZIGGITY BOOM)**
I'm afraid you're not making any sense, Perry.

1956 – ELVIS PRESLEY – **HOUND DOG**
Clearly Elvis had never heard of tautology. Imagine if a dog put out a single titled 'Man Person' – I bet Elvis would have had something to say!

1966 – Norma Tanega – **Walkin' My Cat Named Dog**
That's just wilful stupidity.

1966 – Cat Stevens – **I Love My Dog**
Would have been far more like it, had he not been a man named
Cat. Had possibly been listening to too much Norma Tanega.

1974 – David Bowie – **Diamond Dogs**
As any fool knows, dogs are not made of diamonds. The ingredients
of a dog are as follows: heart, liver, kidneys, fur, tongue,
Corn Flakes, sugar, eyes, greaseproof paper, four yoghurt pots,
head, spam.

1978 – Brian & Michael – **Matchstalk Men And Matchstalk Cats And Dogs**
The UK's one-hit wonder has several glaring errors. (1) It's
'matchstick' not 'matchstalk'. (2) Even assuming their names were
Brian and Michael, was 'Brian and Michael' really the best band
name they could come up with? (3) Why not just call themselves
'Two Men' and have done with it? (4) I bet if they had a dog, they'd
twiddle their thumbs for ages then call it 'Dog'. (5) Mind you, even
that's preferable to Norma Tanega's lunacy.

1980 – Shakin' Stevens – **Hot Dog**
Stop shakin', man, and open the back window of that parked
vehicle! We'll have you for animal cruelty!

1994 – Snoop Doggy Dogg – **Doggy Dogg World**
Blibbly Wibble Wobb.

2000 – Baha Men – **Who Let the Dogs Out?**
There isn't time for recriminations! Get those dogs back indoors!

Famous Dogs in History

2. Laika

The first dog in space. Had other dogs seen what happened to her, she would have been the only dog in space. But there you go – that's Russia for you during the Fifties. Pretty secretive.

Many people – well, everyone really – think that Laika was a Russian dog. She wasn't. She was born Licker, to Cedric and Marcia Smith of Laburnum Way, Croydon, south London, and changed her name to Laika for reasons of authenticity when she became involved in the Soviet space programme.

It happened like this. One winter morning in 1956, little Licker was browsing through *Pravda* while her owners snoozed, and spotted something intriguing in the Small Ads. It read:

> SMALL DOG WANTED. MUST ENJOY OWN COMPANY AND NOT BE AFRAID OF HEIGHTS. OWN HELMET HANDY BUT NOT ESSENTIAL. CALL MOSCOW 003578.

Licker, being an adventurous little dog and slightly irritated by Mr Smith, who drooled more than she did, got on the phone. The next thing she knew, she was being flown to Moscow by Yuri Gagarin, in a private jet. There she met the chief of the Soviet space programme, who noted on seeing the little dog, 'Da. I like her!' And so the name Laika was born. This is all true.

Laika took to weightlessness like a duck to Waltzers. She was sick a lot and complained of headaches. But there was no turning back. At least, not when your kennel is guarded by 17 heavies in furry hats with Kalashnikovs.

And so it came to pass in late 1957 that the plucky little dog was loaded into Sickle 2 and blasted off into space. The Russians maintained that she later returned home safely and was living happily in Murmansk with a harem of gentleman dogs. The truth only emerged decades later that she had died a few hours after launch.

Romantics cling to the belief that Laika's still up there and has turned into a bright star, visible from Croydon on winter nights in the northern sky, halfway between Orion and Cassiopeia. Others say she fell to earth in Nevada and was sold as crisps to locals. We may never know the truth.

Some Dog Sayings and What They Mean

'A KITCHEN-DOG IS NEVER A GOOD RABBIT-HUNTER.'
Rabbits don't tend to congregate in kitchens.

'ONE BARKING DOG SETS THE STREET BARKING.'
Dogs can be really annoying.

'GIVE A DOG A BAD NAME AND HANG HIM.'
Treat dogs really badly.

'HE WHO PELTS EVERY BARKING DOG MUST PICK UP
MANY STONES.'
Treating dogs really badly can be hard work.

'THE HINDMOST DOG MAY CATCH THE HARE.'
It's OK to be lazy.

'A DOG HAS FOUR FEET, BUT HE CAN'T WALK FOUR DIFFERENT PATHS.'
Despite having four legs, dogs can't split themselves into four parts which
each go their separate ways. (Like, duh!)

'WHY KEEP A DOG AND BARK YOURSELF?'
Stop barking – people will think you're simple.

'IF A DOG'S PRAYERS WERE ANSWERED, BONES WOULD RAIN FROM
THE SKY.'
In an emergency situation, don't let your dog do the praying.

'IF IT WERE A DOG, IT WOULD HAVE BITTEN YOU ALREADY.'
That's not a dog, that's a rabbit.

'IF YOU WISH THE DOG TO FOLLOW YOU, FEED HIM.'
Starve your dog before you go out on a hot date.

'YOU CAN'T TEACH AN OLD DOG NEW TRICKS.'
Senility happens to the best of us.

How To... Perform a Risk Assessment

1. Have a good look around.

2. If it seems safe, go to 5.

3. If it could go either way, go to 6.

4. If it seems dangerous, go to 7.

5. Bark loudly while looking pleased with self. Shoot owner a 'Lucky you've got me with you, eh?' look, as if you're responsible for the relative comfort of the situation.

6. Bark loudly while looking as if you're ready to leap into action, when the fact is that you're a coward born into the wrong species. Shoot human companion a 'Do something! You're the one with opposable thumbs and a green belt in judo (although you were flexible and 15 when you won that, and now you're 42 and list "Eating cheese" among your interests!)' look.

7. Bark loudly while peeing self. Run for the hills.

Games Dogs Can Play

2. Soak the Human

This is one of my favourites. It gets them back for all the times they've sneakily lobbed a stick into water and I've gone blindly leaping after it. The only downside is that to transfer water from yourself to a human you first have to get wet yourself. So if you're going to try this game yourself, I recommend doing so near a heated swimming pool. Perhaps one with a Jacuzzi.

1. So they've got the stick, the water's there, and you can see it in their eyes that they have a soaking lined up for you. Go with it.

2. They lob the stick. You follow it. Splash! You're in, paddling – they call it doggy-paddling, to us it's just paddling – for all you're worth. You find the stick, grab it, swim back to dry land.

3. Now you're out. You're looking at them, they're looking at you. It's like *Gunfight at the OK Corral*, except there's no corral and OK doesn't come into it – this is going to be brilliant! (A tip: try growing your hair beforehand, as longer hair retains more water. If anyone accuses you of being a hippie, just stare at them knowingly.)

4. They'll probably spot it in your eyes that you have every intention of shaking your fur near them. At this point, they'll start backing away.

5. Move towards them slowly. They'll probably start jogging. Pick up your pace. They'll start running, probably shouting things like, 'Don't you dare!', 'Please no!' or 'I have a heart condition!' Ignore them.

6. Even if they run to New Zealand, follow them. When they finally give up, probably falling to the ground, set your stall out right beside them and shake, baby, shake! The best part is, it's all a big game so they'll hug you for it afterwards.

Things for Dogs to Build

2. Postman Scarer

Are you a small dog whose bark is less disconcerting than the distant 'ting' of a triangle played by a nervous child named William in a neighbouring junior school?

How many times have you spotted an approaching postman from the lounge window, dashed to the letterbox and yapped through it, causing said postman to be about as scared as a lady suddenly shown some daisies? It's embarrassing, isn't it?

Dogs are supposed to terrorize anyone foolish enough to attempt to deliver the mail – that's our job. Well, fear not, small dogs, your time has come!

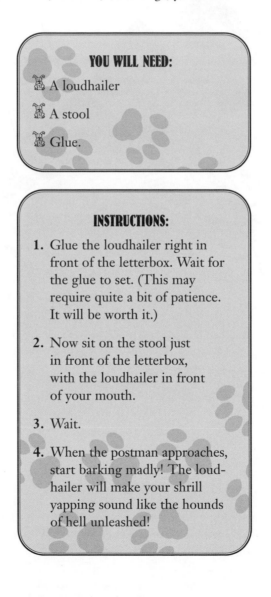

YOU WILL NEED:

🐰 A loudhailer

🐰 A stool

🐰 Glue.

INSTRUCTIONS:

1. Glue the loudhailer right in front of the letterbox. Wait for the glue to set. (This may require quite a bit of patience. It will be worth it.)

2. Now sit on the stool just in front of the letterbox, with the loudhailer in front of your mouth.

3. Wait.

4. When the postman approaches, start barking madly! The loud-hailer will make your shrill yapping sound like the hounds of hell unleashed!

The Six Types of Dog Personality

Some humans say there are five, but they've probably just forgotten one. Most suggest that the six are: Aggressive, Confident, Outgoing, Adaptable, Insecure and Independent. In my experience – which is vast – these tell only part of the story. Here, then, are my Six Types of Dog Personality:

Dog Personality 1:
Dopey

Lies around a lot, generally with saggy chops and floppy ears. When the dopey dog deigns to look around, its eyes say, 'Oh, it's you' in a very slow drawl that threatens to become boring.

TYPICAL DOPEY DOG: **BLOODHOUND.**

DP2: Sneezy

Sneezes a lot. Terrible during the summer season when the pollen count is high. Anyone encountering such a dog during those months is advised to wear a face mask and carry an umbrella.

TYPICAL SNEEZY DOG: **CHIHUAHUA.**

DP3: Bashful

Forever looking coy. All that false modesty can become irritating. 'Oooh, did I really save that small human from drowning?' YES, YOU DID – NOW GET OVER YOURSELF! I've saved small humans from drowning before and no one ever heard the last of it!

TYPICAL BASHFUL DOG: **CAVALIER KING CHARLES SPANIEL.**

DP4: Grumpy

Mind yourself on this one. Nothing's ever good enough. The meat's too dry, the ground's too soft, the rain's too wet, the stick's too wooden, the kennel's too kennel-y… on and on it goes. Steer well clear.

TYPICAL GRUMPY DOG: **THAT POINTER TWO DOORS DOWN.**

DP5: Happy

Think: me. Although I will admit I have my moments!!!!! I'm a crazy kinda guy in a crazy kinda world on a crazy kinda journey just doing my thing!

TYPICAL HAPPY DOG: **YOURS TRULY. (AM IN DANGER OF BECOMING BASHFUL HERE.)**

DP6: Sid

I first met Sid in the autumn of '98 and there was no dog quite like him. What a guy. He could charm the ladies out of their kennels, make a delicious three-course meal from wood and run faster than a cheetah (admittedly a cheetah he had previously weighed down with rocks). If I'd been of a different persuasion… Anyway. I wonder where Sid is now?

TYPICAL SID DOG: **JUST SID. SIGH.**

Dogs to Avoid

There are plenty of hard dogs out there, who we should be scared of. Dobermans, Alsatians, Pit Bull Terriers, Poodles... (That last one might just be a personal thing.)

You can spot them by their ferocious demeanour, but there are other ways to tell them apart from the average mild-mannered pooch like myself:

1. They tend to hang around in gangs, possibly in doorways.

2. They wear hoods and/or baseball caps.

3. They mutter things as you walk past or say things confrontationally, like 'Did you spill my water dish?'

4. They skive off Fetch.

5. Humans don't hold their chains – they do.

6. They wear dog collars. On their legs.

The only way to treat such loutish behaviour is to confront it. Stand up to these dogs. Growl and bare your own tee... Hahahahahahahaha! Sorry, couldn't keep that up.

Run away! Run away! Run away!

Strange Dog Breeds
(What Were They Thinking?)

The dog breeds I am about to list here are 100 per cent genuine. Honestly. We've all heard of Alsatians and Labradors and Poodles, but did you know about Hovawarts and Plotts? I'll never be ashamed to be a Mongrel again.

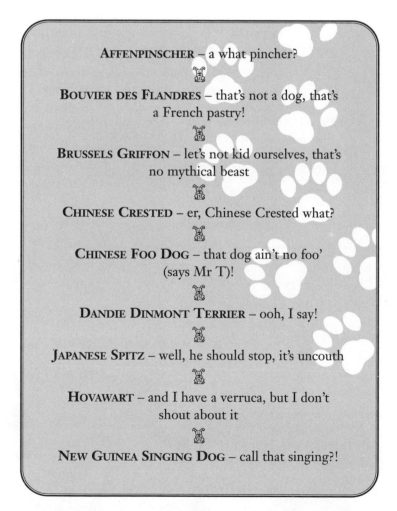

AFFENPINSCHER – a what pincher?

BOUVIER DES FLANDRES – that's not a dog, that's a French pastry!

BRUSSELS GRIFFON – let's not kid ourselves, that's no mythical beast

CHINESE CRESTED – er, Chinese Crested what?

CHINESE FOO DOG – that dog ain't no foo' (says Mr T)!

DANDIE DINMONT TERRIER – ooh, I say!

JAPANESE SPITZ – well, he should stop, it's uncouth

HOVAWART – and I have a verruca, but I don't shout about it

NEW GUINEA SINGING DOG – call that singing?!

NORWEGIAN ELKHOUND – see above

NOVA SCOTIA DUCK TOLLING RETRIEVER – let me get this right, this dog retrieves duck tolls in Nova Scotia?

PAPILLON – nope, that's a butterfly

PETIT BASSET GRIFFON VENDEEN – sorry, you've lost me

PLOTT – Plott? Plott?! The Plott thickens.

All together now: 'What were they thinking?!'

How To... Garner Attention

We all love to be loved. The cuddles, the scratches, the pats, the 'good boy/girl!', the accepting us licking their faces, despite the fact that our tongue germs could wipe out half a nation if packed into a rocket nose cone and fired skywards. It's why we dogs were put on earth: to feel wanted, to feel cherished, to know that our innate desire to be obsequious has not gone unnoticed. We love to be loved.

The problem is, it doesn't always happen. At best, it's a human merely ignoring your imploring gaze. At worst, it's getting trodden on. 'Hell-ooooo! I am down here, you know!'

Do you feel you could be more appreciated? Course you do! All you need to do is remind them you're there. Can't fail to result in a little tender lovin', just cos you're you. So here are my Top Tips for Garnering Attention. Start at number one, and work your way down the list until something sticks...

1. GO DOE-EYED

The very basics. If you can't manage this, you might as well have 'DOOR MAT' tattooed across your forehead. Lower the chin, tilt the head slightly, aim eyes upwards, with a look that says, 'Won't somebody wuv me?'

2. LOOK EXPECTANT

I'd be surprised if they didn't go for 1. Maybe you're in a harsh environment? Just looking like you're expecting something to happen often does the trick. They don't know what it is you're expecting, which makes them feel guilty, which often results in apologetic petting. Try this: pant noisily – use that tongue! – without it sounding like you're making a crank call; appear a little restless; give it some eyes. Come on – who could resist?!

3. GET TACTILE

OK, if they did resist, try the touchy-feely approach. Put a foot in their lap, look imploring. If you can go for the handshake, all the better. Personally, every time I lift one paw, the other three get the fear and I topple over. It ain't dainty. But they love a little ingenuity, the humans. Surely you're in love-land by now?

4. FART

The Last Resort. A smell like last summer's trash sack served with boiled cabbage is guaranteed to attract attention. The trick here is to let them think it's not you. That you've rooted out the culprit and should therefore be showered in gratitude and affection. So it goes like this:

a) Fart (ideally having just eaten last summer's trash sack with boiled cabbage). Be careful to make sure it's silent!

b) Point at Grandpa asleep in his armchair.

c) Whimper.

d) Retreat into the arms of your human companion, as if bonded in adversity.

e) Accept that lovin' gratitude!

f) Join in with a little enthusiastic barking when Grandpa wakes up and everyone turns on him.

Ten Ways to Pass the Time

1. BARK AT THE MOON

Best done at night. Look upwards. That big silver thing, that's the moon. (Don't confuse this with the smaller silver things, which are the stars, or the big orange thing during the day, which is the sun. That ends the astronomy lesson.) Now point snout at moon and bark. No idea what that's all about, but we've been doing it for centuries. It's in our genes.

2. STARE AT FOOD

Whenever a human is eating within eyeshot, pad up to them and sit at their feet, staring at their plate with a 'Can I have some?' look. They may ignore you or perhaps even tell you to go away (possibly more rudely than that). Pay no heed. This is a task requiring patience.

3. JUST LIE AROUND

I know, I know, we dogs aren't very good at Just Lying Around. But give it a shot.

4. THEN LIE AROUND SOME MORE

If you got the hang of 3 after a few attempts, try it again, straight away. You may grow to like it.

5. ADVANCED LYING AROUND

When you become expert at Just Lying Around, practise the Raised Eyes look. The best practitioners of this find they can look around while moving only one or two optical muscles. Practise this until you too have reached a Zen State of Total Lethargy.

6. GO FOR A WALK

Despite possibly being able to get used to Just
Lying Around, we dogs also enjoy exercise. Sadly,
most of us need to be accompanied by a human,
who may also be well-versed in Just Lying Around.
If your human appears to be inert, rouse them
from their laziness by barking, wagging your tail
frantically and poking/pawing them. Failing that,
wee on their feet.

7. FLIRT

While out walking, take every opportunity to
flirt with the opposite sex. If the flirtation is
returned, chew through your leash, grab her/
him and run for the hills together, clutching
contraception gingerly between your teeth. (If
you're too embarrassed to buy contraceptives, a
bucket of cold water usually does the trick.)

8. FEIGN AGGRESSION

Also while walking. If you spot another dog you don't
like the look of, go insane, growling, barking and
straining at the leash, as if you're desperate to get at
them for a big fight. (The fact is, you aren't, you're a
coward, but your humans should keep you apart,
shouting, 'Leave it, he isn't worth it!' Hopefully.)

9. INDULGE IN EXISTENTIAL ANGST

Having scanned my above list, I'm wondering
whether it isn't all slightly pointless. Is this really
a Dog's Life: barking, staring, walking a bit and
Just Lying Around? I'm beginning to feel a
touch guilty in philanthropic terms, so let's put
that right and Do Some Good in the World...

10. FIND A CURE FOR CANCER

This may take a little while, but should pass the
time usefully. If unsure where to start, see 'Things
for Dogs to Build 6: Laboratory' on page 122.

Can Dogs Actually Play Pool?

We've all seen it (and if you haven't I'll describe it shortly, if you can just be a bit patient) – that painting of the dogs playing pool. It's called 'The Hustler'. Six dogs, all different breeds, are gathered round a pool table. They are smoking and drinking. Two of them are playing pool.

Now, let's just dissect this scene for a moment at face value, before we even get into the deeper stuff.

> Two dogs are playing pool while four others spectate. One of the dogs sports a natty waistcoat and is smoking a cigar. There's a Bulldog smoking a cigarette and a Great Dane (wearing a visor, mind) smoking a pipe. One's wearing a bowler hat, the Alsatian's drinking a pint of beer, and the Bassett Hound must be short-sighted, because he's wearing spectacles. Fans of perspective might like to check out the right rear leg of the Bulldog, which, if the painting is to be believed, is as long as a pool table is high.

Let's look at that one more time, before we even begin to get into the opposable-thumbs argument.

> 1. One of the dogs sports a natty waistcoat.
>
> 2. Two of them wear headgear.
>
> 3. Three of them are smoking.
>
> 4. The Alsatian is drinking beer.

5. The Bassett Hound wears spectacles.

6. The Great Dane appears to be standing on one leg.

7. As does the Bulldog taking the shot. An unusually long leg for a Bulldog. Unless it's a very short table. (And everyone knows that you have to keep two feet on the ground in pool. So he's a cheat, as well as having stupid legs.)

None of the above is what you'd term 'generally associated with dogs'.

NOW FOR THE OPPOSABLE-THUMBS BIT:

How exactly is that Bulldog holding the fat end of his cue? Perhaps someone has helpfully glued it to his paw? Perhaps he stood in a stubborn piece of chewing-gum, which is keeping it in place? Perhaps a colony of tics living in his paw have ganged together and are clinging to the cue for dear life, using their teeny-weeny limbs? Perhaps a herd of wildebeest swept majestically across the plains and... no. None of that happened.

Dogs cannot play pool. QED.

Famous Dogs in History

3. Eddie from *Frasier*

I'm stunned. Staggered. It's like someone ripped my food bowl away and replaced it with someone's head. I was always under the assumption that Eddie, the hilarious companion of Martin in *Frasier*, was a Jack Russell Terrier. But I just read a cast list and it ran like this:

FRASIER CRANE	... Kelsey Grammer
NILES CRANE	... David Hyde Pierce
MARTIN CRANE	... John Mahoney
DAPHNE MOON	... Jane Leeves
ROZ DOYLE	... Peri Gilpin
BOB BRISCOE	... Dan Butler
EDDIE	... Moose

Eddie is a moose?!

As far as I was aware... Hang on, what's the plural of moose? Mooses? Meece? I'll go with that. As far as I was aware, meece were vast beasts with rubbery lips and giant horns. So if Eddie is actually a moose, that means that someone must have sawn off his horns, shaved his fur and painted him brown and white.

But it gets more sinister. If Eddie is really about six feet tall, to the shoulder, how tall does that make the human cast?! Kelsey Grammer and co must be actual, real-life giants! Which means the set must be proportionally huge, to make the actors seem normal-sized!

Imagine the actual size of Martin's chair! Sends shivers down your spine.

It's no wonder we haven't seen much of the cast since the sitcom closed. Everything's suddenly falling into place. Mind you, watch out for a remake of *Land of the Giants*, or for Kelsey Grammer in *Jack and the Beanstalk* (not playing Jack, if you get my drift)...

Things for Dogs to Build

3. Tongue Tray

Ever found yourself in posh company and suddenly realized that your tongue is lolling limply from your mouth, like a dishcloth soaked in snail trails, dripping goo that smells like a hermit's sleeping quarters?

It's embarrassing, isn't it? Fear not, I have the perfect gadget for you, invented – and often used – by my good self. I call it: the Tongue Tray. And it does precisely what it says on the tin.

YOU WILL NEED:

A small tray in the shape of your tongue

A lolly stick.

INSTRUCTIONS:

1. Glue the lolly stick to the underside of the tray.

That's it! Now, during special occasions (meetings with VIPs, bar mitzvahs, etc.) insert into mouth.

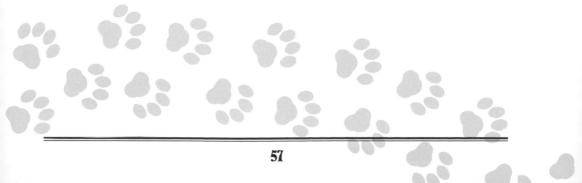

No one said it would be comfortable. But then, good manners come at a cost.

White Doggy-Do - Myth or Reality?

There come tales, once in every blue moon, of the spotting of canine doggy-do that is pure white. White as the driven snow, if somewhat less smooth. Can there be any credence to these tales? Is it possible that a dog can defecate in white? Or are these myths, concocted by those who would spread false word of fanciful faeces?

The first recorded White Doggy-Do tale occurs in 1072, when a census of the land included this entry:

> Mr & Mrs Reg Smythe, 10, The Hovel, London.
> Children: 2 (Grunt, male, Gruntetta, female).
> Luxuries: 2 (Ironing board, Roof). Pets: 5 (2 Chickens,
> 1 Pig, 1 Earwig, 1 Snail). Misc Notes: Spotted what
> looked to be white doggie-do in the kitchen – yet
> the household has no dog! Admittedly might have
> been a hard-boiled egg – I was in a bit of a hurry.

Hardly conclusive. And it's possible the census-taker was several elves short of a grotto. So we come to the next recorded sighting, in William Shakespeare's well-known *Hamlet*:

> **HAMLET**: Alas, poor Yorick…
> Hang on, that isn't… Is it? Can't
> be! … Is that white doggy-do
> before me?
>
> **YORICK:** Don't ask me, I'm just
> a skull.

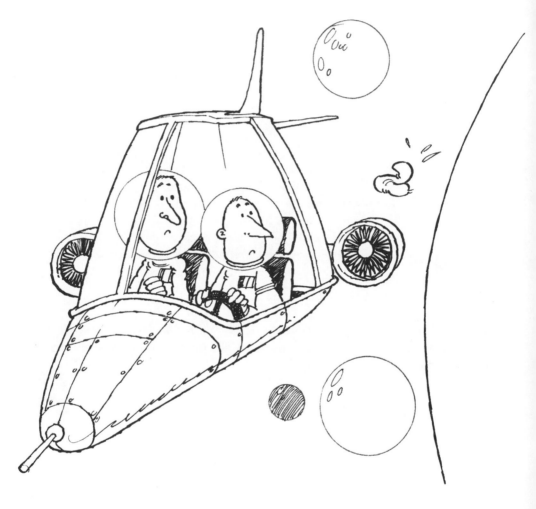

Again, inconclusive. You'll notice that Hamlet isn't entirely certain of what he has witnessed – though whatever it is comes as such a shock to him that he breaks out of iambic pentameter. Yorick is noticeably no help at all. No wonder someone had bumped him off.

Which brings us to 1969 and the moon landing of Apollo 11. Neil Armstrong's speech is the subject of some controversy, but I have listened carefully and I'm pretty sure I heard him say this:

> **ARMSTRONG:** That's one small step for man. One giant leap for mankind. [He begins to walk on the lunar surface.] The surface appears to be very, very fine grain, like a powder. I can kick it loosely with my toes. I can… Wait a minute! I think it might be finely powdered white doggy do! [He kicks at some. We shall never know for certain what it was, since it floated out into space and is currently orbiting Neptune.]

For me, the most compelling story comes from the 1982 biography of the celebrated con artist, Jimmy 'Just Kidding' Kidderminster:

> 'Tricked next-door neighbour Ernie with the old White Doggy-Do Scam. "White dog-sh*t! Amazing!" he exclaimed, before I told him I'd painted his pooch's doings with whitewash…'

Case closed.

TIMOTHY

3. Tree Climbing

Only kidding! I couldn't climb a hill of beans constructed by a toddler named Timothy, and neither could you. Just live with it.

Dangerous Liaisons
(Known to Humans as Crossbreeding
No-No's)

THE WIT TO WOO

Over the page are some potential doggie match-ups that don't even sound wise on paper, let alone in the local park.

For example, St Bernards should always steer clear of Poodles in the romantic sense as this just looks silly… and the consequence could be a St Bernadoodle.

Bearded Collie + Hovawart = **BEARDED WART**

Smooth Fox Terrier + Hovawart

= **SMOOTH WART**

Giant Schnauzer + Hovawart
= **GIANT WART**

Miniature Schnauzer + Cardigan Welsh Corgi
= **MINIATURE CARDIGAN**

Interesting Terrier* + Belgian Malinois
= **INTERESTING BELGIAN**

Spinone Italiano + Gordon Setter
= **SPIN ON IT GORDON**

Brussels Griffon + Rat Terrier + Boerboel
= **BRUSSELS R TERRI-BOEL**

Bearded Collie + Australian Shepherd + Chesapeake
Bay Retriever + Giant Schnauzer + Boxer +
Otterhound + Mastiff
= **BEARDED AUSTRALIAN HESA GIANT B-OTTER-M**

Rottweiler + English Cocker Spaniel
= **ROTT-EN...**

Actually, I think we'll leave it right there. And I haven't even mentioned the Shih Tzu yet.

* MIGHT HAVE MADE THAT ONE UP.

A Shaggy Dog Story

There was once a shaggy dog. He had lots of messy fur. Er. His name was Gerald. Cough. That's all I can think of... The End.

(I have no idea why shaggy dog stories are so popular.)

Famous Dogs in History

4: Nipper

Nipper is the dog in the HMV logo who listens intently to the gramophone. You know the one: slightly cocked head, ear to the trumpet bit. Here's what you didn't know: Nipper was a good friend of Elvis Presley! Stories of how they came to meet litter the history books, so it's hard to know which to believe, but they include:

* Elvis took a shine to the little dog when he spotted the HMV logo and asked to meet him.
* It is said that Elvis tried out his song 'Hound Dog' on an actual dog before releasing it to the public, and that that dog was Nipper, who happened to be walking past the recording studios at the time.
* Elvis got the munchies one day and spotted some food in a bowl – which turned out to be Nipper's. They became friends while fighting over the meaty chunks.

Whatever the truth, the two became firm pals. But their friendship would not last. The problem was that Nipper was an over-enthusiastic little pooch, who did enjoy his rock and roll. So when he accompanied Elvis on his singing tours, he could often not restrict himself to merely watching from the side of the stage. Every so often, he'd invade the stage and start jumping up to yelp into Elvis's microphone, or lick the singer's ears and face while he was trying to sing. Elvis generously lived with the distractions until Nipper took to dry-humping his leg, as little dogs sometimes do. TV stations were obliged to film Elvis above the waist only, since viewers really didn't want to see Nipper clinging to his calves. That proved the final straw for 'The King', who banished the little dog from his entourage.

What happened to Nipper after this, no one can say for sure. When the question is raised today, few dare to mention ol' Elvis's increasing appetite for junk food, or the fact that the little terrier's disappearance coincided with a sudden alarming expansion of the Presley paunch.

Could a Dog Eat Itself to Death?

It has been said – though I have no idea whether it is true – that a dog left alone with way too much food will eat itself to death. That it has no mechanism for telling itself when it is full.

I know I'm partial to treats, but I know when to stop… Actually, that's not true. I reckon if you left me with enough beef crisps to fill a dustbin, I would scoff the lot. Then I would track down the beef crisps factory and break into that under the cover of darkness, and I would eat all the beef crisps in the beef crisps factory. After the beef crisps-makers had discovered the crime, and made a fresh new batch of beef crisps, I would break in again and eat all those crisps, until they finally invented a security system I could not crack.

Assuming by that stage that I had eaten the country's entire supply of beef crisps, I would buy up thousands of bags of plain crisps and I would go into a field of cows and I would rub the crisps against the cows, and I would eat all of those. After that, I would feel a bit sick and would go off beef crisps.

Anyway, that's just a little recurring nightmare of mine.

In case you are not as disciplined as me food-wise, here is my Handy Visual Guide to Knowing When You Have Eaten Enough. To use it, scoff in front of a mirror, comparing yourself to the two pictures as you do so.

A healthy diet   'Stop eating, you fat git!'

The Worst Thing in the World: You're a Cute Small Dog and You've Just Been Bought By a Young Lady Celebrity

I thank heaven that I'm pretty much the size of a dustbin, and as attractive (and hygienic) to boot, because it means I've absolutely no chance of being hoisted under the arm of Paris Hilton.

> ## BEWARE PURCHASE BY ANY YOUNG LADY CELEB (YLC)
>
> The next thing you know, they've blow-dried your tail, stuffed you into a pink D&G jumpsuit – even though you're a dog and, to the best of your knowledge, haven't written 'Go parachuting' anywhere in your diary – perfumed your nether regions, named you Princess Fifi Foofoobelle – even though you're a gentleman – and now your head's poking out of a designer bag the size of China and you're being snapped by paparazzi, while wearing a Burberry ribbon in your hair. THE GUT-CLAWING SHAME!

It gets worse. Now your YLC has met up with other YLCs (consider Lindsay Lohan, Victoria Beckham, that sort of thing) – and they're talking to each other. Great, wafting clouds of vacuity, floating around your head. If one of those clouds lands on you, you'll be swallowed like a spaceship in a black hole and be transported

to a land where a golden shoe with a very high heel is God and everyone gets a recording contract even if they sound like a gibbon suspended over a chasm by a man trying to scrape the paint off a chalkboard using polystyrene shaped like a rictus grin. IT'S THAT BAD.

And you know the problem? We dogs are so nice, we won't do anything about it. We'll sit in that bag, yapping to order, patiently modelling doggy-nappies and occasionally nodding in agreement when Lohan makes a point about the comfort of slingbacks.

I say this: Cute Small Dogs, rise up! Here's what to do:

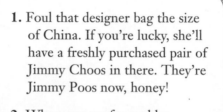

1. Foul that designer bag the size of China. If you're lucky, she'll have a freshly purchased pair of Jimmy Choos in there. They're Jimmy Poos now, honey!

2. Whenever confronted by paparazzi, reach out and lick the lens of your YLC's sunglasses, having only very recently chewed spinach, curry sauce, octopus and sheep's testicles*.

3. When your YLC plays her latest single to you and asks what you think of it, throw yourself out of the nearest window, screaming.

Soon enough, you'll be back at the Pooch Parlour and she'll be looking for a new sucker.

* IF YOU CAN'T FIND SHEEP'S TESTICLES, MEATBALLS WILL DO.

Things for Dogs to Build

4. Scooby Scoop

I've named this after the celebrated cartoon Great Dane, Scooby-Doo, who is well-known for shovelling ludicrous amounts of food into his gob in one go. Because that's what we're aiming to do! Why spend ages chewing politely when you could inhale food like a vacuum cleaner, leaving plenty of time free to beg for more?

YOU WILL NEED:

🐾 JCB

🐾 Lots of Food

🐾 JCB Operator.

INSTRUCTIONS:

1. Using the JCB and JCB Operator, scoop up the Lots of Food.

2. Wait expectantly under the scoop with your mouth open.

3. Loft a thumb, signalling the JCB Operator to tip the treats…

4. Eat your way out of that lot. (May take some time.)

Origins of the Phrase 'Man's Best Friend is His Dog'

This one actually started with Adam and Eve. Everyone knows that in the Garden of Eden there was the first man (Adam), the first woman (Eve), a serpent (snake) and a tree. What they don't know is that there was also the first dog (Dennis).

HERE'S WHAT ACTUALLY HAPPENED:

Every morning, Adam and Eve would wake up and think to themselves, 'This Garden of Eden's a bit of all right! We are happy here.' Immediately, the snake would put a spanner in the works by trying to tempt the couple into eating an apple, which they knew they shouldn't do. Dennis would happily have eaten the apple, but it was in a tree and he wasn't very good at climbing.

One morning, while Adam's elsewhere, the snake cajoles Eve into taking the apple and holding it in her hands. She stares at it and thinks it looks very juicy and delicious. Dare she eat it?

Eve's just about to scoff the apple when she has a pang of guilt and tosses it quickly away. It lands right at the feet of Dennis, who doesn't think twice. He launches himself at the fruit and takes a huge bite. But what's this? There's only a maggot in it. Eugh! Dennis spits out the fruit and eyes Eve angrily. Feeding him grub-infested fruit?! How dare she?

After that, Dennis only ever cosied up to Adam. Whenever Eve went to stroke Dennis, he'd sidle away, scowling disdainfully. Gradually, the animosity became mutual. Eve once even kicked out at Dennis in frustration, but since no one had invented football yet, or allowed girls to take part, she missed.

And that's how the phrase came about. It's not 'Man' as in 'Humankind', more 'Man' as gender-specific, since Eve couldn't abide Dennis and vice versa.

'Whose Best Friend?'

Some of my acquaintances take the oft-used phrase 'Man's best friend is his dog' to be a compliment. It ain't! (I know this hurts, but I've been around the block a few times, trust me.)

So let's look at some other options:

FIRST, KNOW THAT A MAN'S BEST FRIEND IS

▼

His beer

▼

Then his girlfriend

▼

Then the TV remote control

▼

Then lying in his own dribble.

Failing those, let's look at some other options.

'MAN'S BEST FRIEND IS HIS KOMODO DRAGON'?

Nope.

'MAN'S BEST FRIEND IS HIS WESTERN LOWLAND GORILLA'?

Nope.

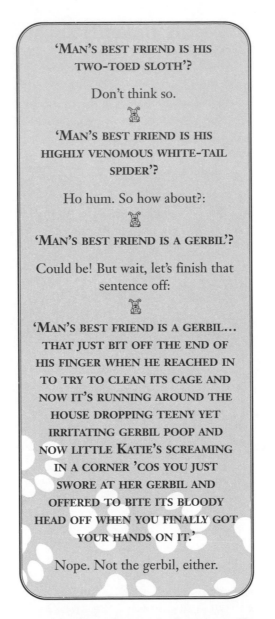

'MAN'S BEST FRIEND IS HIS TWO-TOED SLOTH'?

Don't think so.

'MAN'S BEST FRIEND IS HIS HIGHLY VENOMOUS WHITE-TAIL SPIDER'?

Ho hum. So how about?:

'MAN'S BEST FRIEND IS A GERBIL'?

Could be! But wait, let's finish that sentence off:

'MAN'S BEST FRIEND IS A GERBIL… THAT JUST BIT OFF THE END OF HIS FINGER WHEN HE REACHED IN TO TRY TO CLEAN ITS CAGE AND NOW IT'S RUNNING AROUND THE HOUSE DROPPING TEENY YET IRRITATING GERBIL POOP AND NOW LITTLE KATIE'S SCREAMING IN A CORNER 'COS YOU JUST SWORE AT HER GERBIL AND OFFERED TO BITE ITS BLOODY HEAD OFF WHEN YOU FINALLY GOT YOUR HANDS ON IT.'

Nope. Not the gerbil, either.

See, there are not many animals as nice or obedient as us. You wouldn't catch the average kangaroo nipping into the kitchen to fetch Dad's pipe and slippers. Even if that 'roo were to pick them up, him being inquisitive about pipes and slippers, he'd be off out the door and bouncing down the highway like someone comfortable on springs, with Dad in hot pursuit. And when the animal finally drops them, Dad wheezing at the rear, he's travelled 2.3 miles. The distance from the armchair to the kitchen and back being 17 feet, Dad's just jogged 993.88 times the distance he would have mooched had he fetched the slippers himself.

No, 'Man's best friend is his dog' is used so commonly (despite him preferring beer to us) because we just can't help being so darned nice, and they love a bit of loyalty. In recompense for this obsequiousness we get free treats, so it's not all bad.

'MAN'S BEST FRIEND IS HIS WESTERN LOWLAND GORILLA'?

Everything You Ever Needed to Know About Crufts (and Dog Shows in General)

Crufts is a prestigious annual British dog show, for the type of dog that we genuine mutts hate. It's all, 'Ooh, look at me!', prancing around like the great I-Am. All that lapdog obedience and 'Musical Canine Freestyle'. If dogs were meant to dance to music, they'd have been born with a Bee Gees album in their paws, headbands around their ears and a handbag between their legs. If you ever catch me dancing, tie me to a steam train and pelt me with cacti.

There are several events, the highlight being Best in Show, and some four million pure-bred dogs, or thereabouts, take part each year. These events include such irresistible delights as:

> Walking Around on Tiptoe, Looking Down One's Nose at Other Dogs
>
> Being as Fluffy as Possible
>
> Wondering What's for Tea but Pretending to be Aloof from Hunger
>
> Doing the Daintiest Poo
>
> Accompanying Princes William and Harry for Cocktails.

What a lot of faffing about! On show days, that uppity Poodle across the road is woken at 3.00 am, then they clip him, clop him, primp and groom him until he looks like a shaved baboon. I've watched Crufts on telly – I was dragged along to the show itself once; luckily the doorman stopped me and told me my paws looked like old trainers, so we got kicked out – and it's a terrible embarrassment to the species.

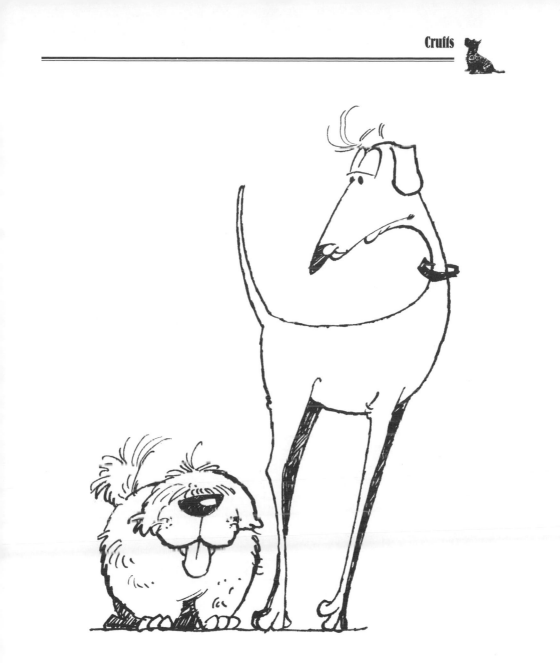

It's the *subservience* of it all that grates the most. Sure, it's good to play the game, just to con treats out of humans, but do wc really need to be so blatant about it?

Take that Accompanying Princes William and Harry for Cocktails event. I've even seen bulldogs – if you please! – giving it the 'Actually, I'm a corgi' look. Makes you sick.

And the snobbery! Let's look at the remarkable names of some of the recent Best in Show winners:

2008: Fotherington-Smythe's Bolt From The Blue Nice Conservatory

2007: Is That An Ozwald Boateng?

2006: Mine's A Caerphilly, Cheese If You Please III

2005: Scarf & Gloves Winter Combination, Oh I Say What a Lovely Hat

2004: Be Thankful I Don't Speak My Mind, Grayson.

I mean! What's so wrong with Jason?!

Dog shows are just wrong. I'm off to eat 14 bowls of Stuff We've Swept Up That Dogs Might Just Eat from the local grot-market, then I'm going to topple into a pond. Stitch that, Mr Cruft!

A Suggested Alternative to Crufts

Crufts and their ilk seek to promote and reward the peak of canine accomplishment. But what about the rest of us? Don't we deserve a trophy or something for just being us? So I've come up with my own doggy awards show, for the lowlier pooch. I call it…

Wuffs

WORST IN SHOW

The highlight of the event. The one they all aspire to. The judges will be looking especially for:

- Slovenly behaviour
- Untidiness
- Matting of fur
- Malodorous drool
- BO
- Greening of tongue
- Missing ear parts
- General disobedience (through lethargy rather than malice)
- A bottom you wouldn't approach wearing a spacesuit.

Should the competition result in a tie, fleas will be counted. The competitor with the greatest number is declared the winner.

The winner receives the Wuffs Worst in Show tin medal. If they can be bothered to collect it.

DOG UNCO-ORDINATION

Why is anyone impressed when a dog can jump through a hoop? It would be far funnier if they missed the hoop altogether, fell on their nose and rolled into an advertising hoarding. With this in mind, the course will involve:

- Some hoops – points awarded for missing hoop, landing on nose, rolling into advertising hoarding. Bonus point for actually landing on the hoop and becoming stuck while draped over it

- A tunnel – points awarded for bumping into mouth of tunnel, missing tunnel altogether, getting lost in tunnel and staying there for ages looking bewildered

- A seesaw – points awarded for missing seesaw, falling off seesaw, catapulting self into crowd

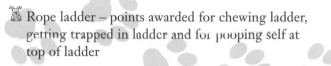

🐾 Rope ladder – points awarded for chewing ladder, getting trapped in ladder and for pooping self at top of ladder

🐾 Ten-foot wall – points awarded for not leaping high enough, thus bouncing off wall to land in dejected heap. Bonus point for each repeat performance

🐾 Slalom poles – points awarded for staring at this part of the course with a 'What do you think I am? A snake?' look.

DISOBEDIENCE

Speaks for itself. Various commands will be uttered:

> 🐾 Sit!
>
> 🐾 Stand!
>
> 🐾 Stay!
>
> 🐾 Here!
>
> 🐾 Wander about a bit!
>
> 🐾 Eat a hat!
>
> 🐾 Learn to speak Spanish!
>
> 🐾 Bark the tune to 'Yesterday'
>   by The Beatles.

The judges will award points to competitors doing the complete opposite of what is asked of them.

How To... Play Dead

🐕 Find another dog that is dead.

🐕 See how it behaves.

🐕 Do that.

Games Dogs Can Play

4. Run Away!

This one is genius. I don't know how I thought of it, but consider it a moment of enlightenment. Here's how you play:

> You run towards a human and then, at the last moment, just as you're about to reach their outstretched arms – you ready for this, the twist in the tail? – you run away! Brilliant!

I'll run that past you again, in case it's too much to take in.

> You run towards a human and then, at the last moment, just as you're about to reach their outstretched arms… you run away!

All right! Everyone repeat with me…

> You run towards a human and then, at the last moment, just as you're about to reach their outstretched arms… Everyone?
>
> **YOU RUN AWAY!**

I know. If I could patent mere actions, I would. Look, here it is in picture form, in case you're still confused:

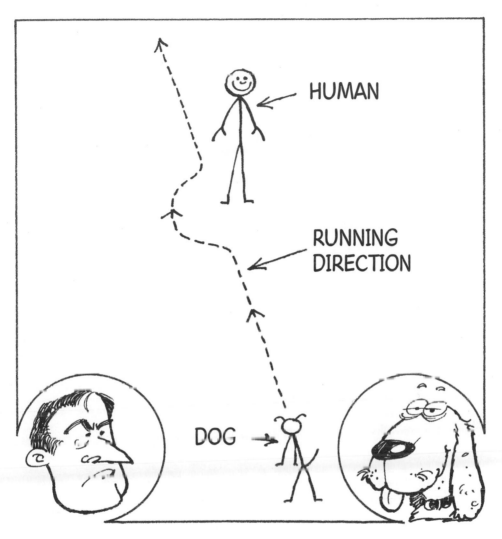

So you keep repeating that, over and over again, because it's such amazing fun. Until, admittedly, the human gets bored and says, 'Oh sod off then.' But it's great until that bit.

No, don't thank me.

NB: Run Away! can also be incorporated into the game of Fetch, which simply requires a stick/ball/etc to be carried in the mouth.

Girl Dogs

Girl dogs are quite different from boy dogs. For a start, they pee differently. They're less likely to snarl at a passing squirrel or to try to rip the throat out of the family chicken. They're more composed than that. When a girl dog needs to pass wind, she goes into the bathroom, she emits the redundant gasses, wags her tail to dispense the odour and returns whence she came as if nothing untoward had happened.

I remember farting once and clearing a medium-sized outdoor park.

So, what does the boy dog do to secure the affections of a girl dog? Here are some handy Don'ts, derived from my years of valuable experience:

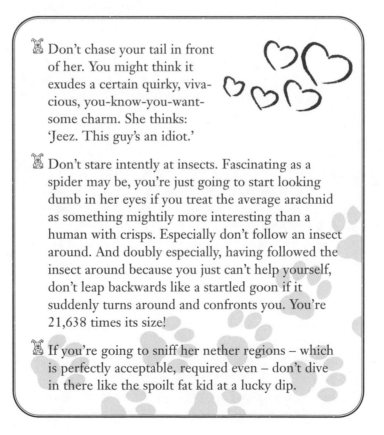

🐾 Don't chase your tail in front of her. You might think it exudes a certain quirky, vivacious, you-know-you-want-some charm. She thinks: 'Jeez. This guy's an idiot.'

🐾 Don't stare intently at insects. Fascinating as a spider may be, you're just going to start looking dumb in her eyes if you treat the average arachnid as something mightily more interesting than a human with crisps. Especially don't follow an insect around. And doubly especially, having followed the insect around because you just can't help yourself, don't leap backwards like a startled goon if it suddenly turns around and confronts you. You're 21,638 times its size!

🐾 If you're going to sniff her nether regions – which is perfectly acceptable, required even – don't dive in there like the spoilt fat kid at a lucky dip.

You're going to have a job chatting her up afterwards if your nose is somewhere among her kidneys. (It once took three humans to wrench my head free from a lady's bottom.)

Don't try to show you're hard by picking a fight with other male dogs, to impress her. You'll end up with egg on your face – literally in my case, when a Chihuahua owner lobbed half a dozen at me from her shopping, after I got aggressive with her little 'Diddums'.

Don't refer to her as a bitch. You're not a rap artist.

Coin Tricks

These are great fun and a perfect way to amaze your friends and family. And they're so simple. All you need is:

A COIN!

So, here we go. This is called the French Drop. Hold the coin by the edge… Ah, I've just spotted the flaw in this plan.

Things for Dogs to Build

5. Boomerang

I've no idea why no dog thought of this before. The boomerang – it's the stick that comes back of its own accord! As in Fetch, without the dog! Geddit?!

YOU WILL NEED:

- One small length of wood
- Hacksaw
- Chisel
- Mallet
- Sandpaper
- Varnish
- Dexterity
- Patience.

Hmm, having just written out that list, I'm beginning to see why no dog *did* think of this before. However, bear with me.

INSTRUCTIONS:

1. Mark a boomerang shape on your length of wood with a pencil. (Seems I forgot 'Pencil' in my list, which is the least of your worries.)

2. Saw out the shape with a hacksaw.

3. Whittle it down using the chisel and
mallet until it looks aerodynamic.

4. Sandpaper to a smooth finish.

5. Varnish and leave to dry.

Now, when your owner suggests a game of Fetch and you can't really be bothered, sneakily swap his actual stick with your boomerang version. The confusion on their face will be priceless! (As will your lovely boomerang be if an art dealer ever finds out a dog made it.)

Doggy Horoscopes - What Your Star Sign Says About You

Each of us is born under a star sign, which determines exactly how we behave, our likes, dislikes and favourite treat, etc. I, Mystic Jace, have consulted the stars and have compiled this handy guide for you...

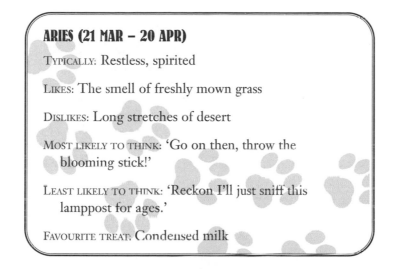

ARIES (21 MAR – 20 APR)

TYPICALLY: Restless, spirited

LIKES: The smell of freshly mown grass

DISLIKES: Long stretches of desert

MOST LIKELY TO THINK: 'Go on then, throw the blooming stick!'

LEAST LIKELY TO THINK: 'Reckon I'll just sniff this lamppost for ages.'

FAVOURITE TREAT: Condensed milk

TAURUS (21 APR – 21 MAY)

TYPICALLY: Stubborn, single-minded

LIKES: Ironing

DISLIKES: Spectating dangerous motorcycle stunts

MOST LIKELY TO THINK: 'No, we'll do it my way.'

LEAST LIKELY TO THINK: 'All right, let's do it your way.'

FAVOURITE TREAT: Wafer biscuits

GEMINI (22 MAY – 21 JUN)

TYPICALLY: Bright, communicative

LIKES: Barking in a knowledgeable manner

DISLIKES: Being referred to as Reg

MOST LIKELY TO THINK: 'You don't want to do it like that!'

LEAST LIKELY TO THINK: 'Silence! Phew! Let's keep it that way!'

FAVOURITE TREAT: Pork sausages

CANCER (22 JUN – 23 JUL)

TYPICALLY: Emotional, aggressive

LIKES: Walking sideways while waving things

DISLIKES: Whispering into the night

MOST LIKELY TO THINK: 'I'll bite the butt off anyone who says there's something wrong with walking sideways!'

LEAST LIKELY TO THINK: 'Perhaps I should calm down a bit.'

FAVOURITE TREAT: BBQ ribs

LEO (24 JUL – 23 AUG)

TYPICALLY: Proud, stubborn

LIKES: Wearing a false beard

DISLIKES: Having to pick the gristly bits out of cheap dog food

MOST LIKELY TO THINK: 'I'm great!'

LEAST LIKELY TO THINK: 'You're great!'

FAVOURITE TREAT: Caviar sandwiches

VIRGO (24 AUG – 23 SEP)

TYPICALLY: Pragmatic, sneaky

LIKES: Granting three wishes to children with shiny lanterns

DISLIKES: Sexual advances

MOST LIKELY TO THINK: 'Not today, thank you, I'm a Virgo!'

LEAST LIKELY TO THINK: 'Whoargh – I'll have a slice of that!'

FAVOURITE TREAT: Unsalted peanuts

LIBRA (24 SEP – 23 OCT)

TYPICALLY: Charming, co-operative

LIKES: Helping old ladies across the road, complimenting them on their choice of hat

DISLIKES: Realizing how far away Tipperary is

MOST LIKELY TO THINK: 'I'll never make it to Tipperary!'

LEAST LIKELY TO THINK: 'I might pop over to Tipperary today!'

FAVOURITE TREAT: Chocolate biscuits

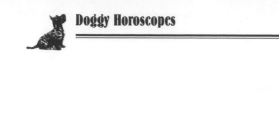

SCORPIO (24 OCT – 22 NOV)

TYPICALLY: Emotional, possessive

LIKES: Kidnapping ex-lovers and keeping them locked in a shed

DISLIKES: The cops

MOST LIKELY TO THINK: 'I have a cunning plan!'

LEAST LIKELY TO THINK: 'I'll never get away with this!'

FAVOURITE TREAT: Porridge

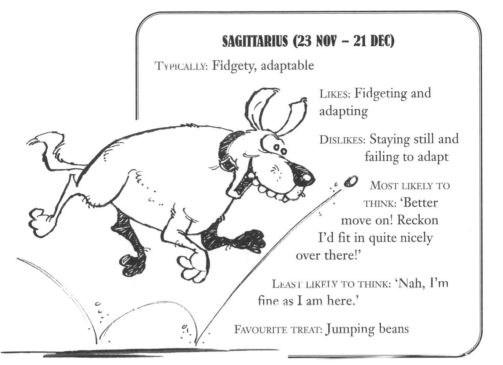

SAGITTARIUS (23 NOV – 21 DEC)

TYPICALLY: Fidgety, adaptable

LIKES: Fidgeting and adapting

DISLIKES: Staying still and failing to adapt

MOST LIKELY TO THINK: 'Better move on! Reckon I'd fit in quite nicely over there!'

LEAST LIKELY TO THINK: 'Nah, I'm fine as I am here.'

FAVOURITE TREAT: Jumping beans

CAPRICORN (22 DEC – 20 JAN)

TYPICALLY: Driven, multi-tasking

LIKES: Christmas, snow, baubles, presents, Santa

DISLIKES: Boxing Day

MOST LIKELY TO THINK: 'Er, where's my present?'

LEAST LIKELY TO THINK: 'That's quite enough presents, thanks.'

FAVOURITE TREAT: Christmas cake and turkey (not Brussels sprouts)

AQUARIUS (20 JAN – 19 FEB)

TYPICALLY: Ideological, principled

LIKES: Listening to *2112* by Rush

DISLIKES: Having to wear a helmet

MOST LIKELY TO THINK: 'The development of modern industry… cuts from under its feet the very foundation on which the bourgeoisie produces and appropriates products.'

LEAST LIKELY TO THINK: 'I love toffs!'

FAVOURITE TREAT: Stew

PISCES (20 FEB – 20 MAR)

TYPICALLY: Introverted, shy

LIKES: Grating cheese

DISLIKES: Training grizzly bears to dance

MOST LIKELY TO THINK: 'Hey, everyone, I'm over he...
Nah, that's just not me.'

LEAST LIKELY TO THINK: 'Great – a loudhailer!'

FAVOURITE TREAT: Oat Crunch breakfast cereal

Exploiting the Reward System

We're dogs and we love to be loved. (As did David Bowie's Jean Genie, but that's another story.) Humans know this and use it to their advantage. Like when they're 'training' us, for instance.

When we do something they want us to do, they treat us which makes them feel good about themselves and makes us feel good about them too. Pats and hugs are to be applauded, something verbal ('Good boy/girl!' etc.) is reasonable, but of course treats are the best. Mmm… treats. Personally, I love Mars bars, toffee apples and beef crisps.

Here's the funny part: humans think they're putting one over on us. All that obedience in return for some minor affection. It doesn't actually work like that.

If one dog can jump through hoops, don't humans realize that all dogs could do the same? Of course we could! (If we wanted to…) We either choose not to because we're stubborn or lazy, or because we haven't been given the confidence in our own abilities.

If I wanted to, I could wash dishes with one paw and conduct the Berlin Philharmonic with the other. I don't for two reasons:

1. I don't like washing up or classical music.

2. If I did, can you imagine what I'd be expected to do next?! Mow the lawn, write a book about Engelbert Humperdinck, conduct tests on trace elements in saliva, perform an entertaining shadow-puppet play about a princess and a dragon for small humans… I'd be on the go constantly!

No, I choose to do nothing more than sitting and staying put when told, because if I do that I get treats. Imagine if I started making my human companions a packed lunch and driving them to work. Do you think I'd get free treats for occasionally sitting down a bit then? Not likely! So I exploit the reward system. And if you aren't already doing the same, you should.

SOME RULES:

1. Be lazy

2. Play hard to get

3. For every action there is an
   equal and opposite reaction.*

* I THINK ISAAC NEWTON MIGHT HAVE SLIPPED THAT ONE IN WHEN I WASN'T LOOKING.

Pooch Parlours
(and How To Avoid Them)

Lady-dogs might like them – and even then that is a rather large generalization – but they are certainly not for us men. Here's why:

Before   **After**

The Devil's work, clearly.

If we were meant to be that well-groomed, we'd have been born with brushes on our paws and deodorant up our butts. Or as cats. (Shudder.) Personally, I love getting messy. I remember making friends with a pair of pigs on a farm one day, and when my human companions found us I was so gloriously filthy they took one of the pigs home by mistake. Which was fine for me until I was expected to roll in my own poo.

So how do you avoid being dragged to your local Pooch Parlour?

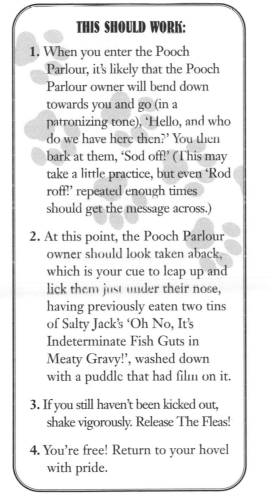

THIS SHOULD WORK:

1. When you enter the Pooch Parlour, it's likely that the Pooch Parlour owner will bend down towards you and go (in a patronizing tone), 'Hello, and who do we have here then?' You then bark at them, 'Sod off!' (This may take a little practice, but even 'Rod roff!' repeated enough times should get the message across.)

2. At this point, the Pooch Parlour owner should look taken aback, which is your cue to leap up and lick them just under their nose, having previously eaten two tins of Salty Jack's 'Oh No, It's Indeterminate Fish Guts in Meaty Gravy!', washed down with a puddle that had film on it.

3. If you still haven't been kicked out, shake vigorously. Release The Fleas!

4. You're free! Return to your hovel with pride.

Games Dogs Can Play

5. Treasure Hunt

All we dogs love to bury things and then dig them up. Sure, it's fun, but generally we're finding things that we put in the ground ourselves. Where's the surprise? It's hardly Christmas, is it?

So I got to thinking. Who else likes to bury things? Anyone?

> 'Yes, you, slow puppy at the back…
> Speak louder! "Undertakers?"'

Right, yes, undertakers *do* like to bury things, but dead humans weren't the sort of surprise I was after. Yes, I know they have lots of bones, but that's just wrong. No.

Anyone else?

No? How about a clue, then?

A-HAR JIM LAD!

All right, here's another:

PIECES OF EIGHT! PIECES OF EIGHT!

Come on, everyone, it's easy! One last clue:

SHIVER ME TIMBERS!

The answer's pirates! Pirates!'

Right, dear reader, it's just you and me. You, me and the brilliant game of Treasure Hunt! Which I invented. Ish.

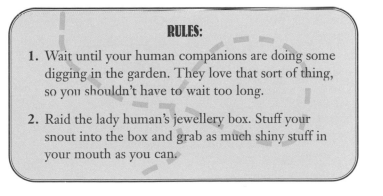

RULES:

1. Wait until your human companions are doing some digging in the garden. They love that sort of thing, so you shouldn't have to wait too long.

2. Raid the lady human's jewellery box. Stuff your snout into the box and grab as much shiny stuff in your mouth as you can.

3. Here's the tricky bit. Wander past your human companions as innocently as possible.

4. Now, when they're not looking, face away from the digging site and fling your head backwards, opening your mouth as you do so. The shiny stuff should arc backwards into the soil.

5. Hope they don't spot it.

6. Wait until the soil has been dug over and return to the scene.

7. Dig it all up, trying to find shiny stuff. This may involve you destroying a new vegetable patch. Just think to yourself: would a pirate feel guilty? No, he wouldn't! Keep digging.

SO FAR, I HAVE LOST/MISLAID:

🐾 1 gold chain

🐾 2 watches

🐾 1 brooch (which her mother gave her, as she told me 18 times)

🐾 7 earrings

🐾 2 gold bands

🐾 1 ruby engagement ring

🐾 1 bracelet (lucky charm – clearly didn't work for her!).

AND I HAVE GONE WITHOUT:

🐾 23 dinners

🐾 Umpteen treats.

Was it worth it? Oh yes.

Faking It

Here's a fun game to play for any household dog whose life occasionally feels mundane. Pretend you're more important than you are! Here are some good examples to follow:

Faking It... As a Sheepdog

YOU WILL NEED:

🐰 Some sheep

🐰 A human with a long, crooked stick who's good at whistling

Wander into the field, looking as if you know what you're doing. I'm not entirely sure what that involves.

I do know that sheepdogs move sheep in a certain direction. How, I have zip idea. The shepherd whistles and shouts commands, depending upon where they want you to stand.

Ignore the whistles and shouts, as you won't have a clue what they're about. Instead, walk ahead of the sheep sneakily dropping ovine snacks as you go. They'll start following you wherever you lead, and the shepherd will be none the wiser.

Shepherd 0 – You 1! Brilliant.

Faking It... As a Gundog

YOU WILL NEED:

🐾 Humans with guns

🐾 Birds.

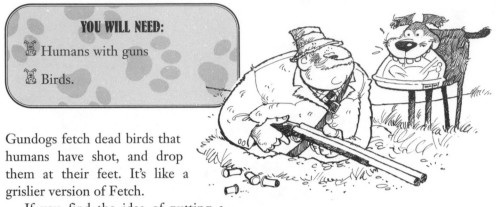

Gundogs fetch dead birds that humans have shot, and drop them at their feet. It's like a grislier version of Fetch.

If you find the idea of putting a still-warm, bloodied bird in your mouth slightly distasteful, I recommend first buying a box of fried chicken and hiding it in the killing ground.

Every time a bird's shot, nip out to that, pick out a chicken piece and take that to the human instead. It might not be the exact creature they shot, but what idiot's going to turn down a delicious piece of fried chicken?

Faking It... As a Greyhound

YOU WILL NEED:

🐾 To be able to run a lot quicker than you can at the moment.

Start by jogging for ten minutes a day and doing a few star jumps. Graduate to press-ups and weights. After a month, alternate jogs and sprints with pole-vaulting and perhaps some discus. By the end of the year, you should be ready to compete with the greyhounds. On the day of the race, remember to take plenty of water and a heart monitor.

Faking It... As a Guard Dog

YOU WILL NEED:

🐾 To be an awful lot scarier than you are at the moment

🐾 A 'Beware of the Dog' sign.

The Chihuahuas and Bichon Frises among you might like to skip this section altogether. The best you can hope for is that the sign will scare intruders off long before they've caught a glimpse of you.

So try the sign. If that fails, I recommend my patented Postman Scarer (see 'Things for Dogs to Build 2: Postman Scarer' on page 37), which should work with intruders as well as postmen.

If that fails, hide.

Faking It... As a Police Dog

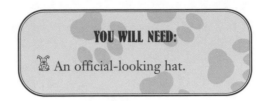

YOU WILL NEED:

🐕 An official-looking hat.

Bark a lot. Even if nothing bad's happening.

In the unfortunate event that you're required to chase an armed raider, with the intention of wrestling them to the ground and disarming them, start limping and stare at your officer with an 'I think I've hurt my foot' look.

You might just get away with it.

Faking It... As a Sled-Dog

YOU WILL NEED:

🐕 To be impervious to the cold

🐕 To have the stamina of an ox

🐕 To consider jogging for ages while pulling several times your own body-weight in snow and ice to be the height of fun...

Actually, I'd stick with one of the other five.

Dog Odour

Any idea why we dogs sniff each other's bottoms? It's because either side of our bottom are glands that secrete a pretty sexy 'Hey everyone! It's me! Come and get some!' odour.

Some of that rubs off on our Number Twos each time we go to the toilet, which is why we also (admittedly) sniff each other's poo.

Now, by the way that humans wrinkle their noses and go 'Eugh!' and that sort of thing, I know they find some of this stuff distasteful. But it ain't to us! Horses for Courses, as they say. Or indeed, Dogs for Poo.

Here are some things *I* find distasteful about *humans*:

- They hog the sofa
- They eat vegetables
- They wear hats
- And trousers
- They take baths
- They think Lassie is great
- They throw sticks but won't fetch them themselves
- They hoard poo! In farms! (Whoever thought of sewage farms!)
- They have sex in front of us and think we're not offended.

Gross.

Famous Dogs in History

5. Cerberus (or Why Stubby-tailed Dogs Should Look Pleased With Themselves)

The three-headed devil-dog of Greek mythology, whose tail was a deadly snake and who hung out in the underworld. The story goes that Cerberus was captured by Heracles/Hercules during the last of his 12 Labours. That isn't true. Here's what really happened.

Cerberus was the only dog of his time who didn't chase his tail. In fact, his tail chased him! (It being a deadly snake.)

While Cerberus was a mere puppy, this didn't present any problems. However, as Charon (who ran the underworld) fed him, he grew – as did his tail (a deadly snake, remember). And one day the tail grew so long that it chased Cerberus around in anticlockwise circles and managed to nip the nose of the devil-dog's right head. The head died and eventually fell off.

The next day, the snake chased Cerberus around in a clockwise direction, nipping the nose of the left head. That too died and eventually fell off. Which left one head, formerly central, which was just out of reach of the annoying deadly tail-snake. But it wouldn't be long before Charon fed it just enough delicious rats for it to grow enough to be able to nip the remaining head on the nose.

The remaining head had some serious thinking to do. One night it came up with a cunning plan. While the deadly tail-snake slept, it crept into Charon's larder and ate all the rats itself. Brilliant! Except that Charon had 23,672 rats stored in there, which was a lot of dead rats to eat in one night.

The following morning, when Charon explained that someone had eaten all the rats in his larder, the deadly tail-snake sussed what must have happened, particularly as the remaining head was groaning a lot and looked quite pale.

So the deadly talking snake taunted the remaining head: 'Could I interest you in just one wafer-thin slice of rat, remaining head?' he hissed.

'Naff off, I'm stuffed,' replied the remaining head. Then Cerberus exploded, scattering dog bits all over the earth. And everywhere a dog bit landed, a new dog grew – with barely a tail, since the last one had proved so annoying.

So, all you dogs with silly nubby tails out there, take heart in the fact that you are genuinely descended from the original devil-dog himself, Cerberus!

Digby - A Timely Re-evaluation

According to the popular British documentary of 1973 – fondly remembered by those old enough and gullible enough to be taken in – Digby was the Biggest Dog in the World. Hmm.

Right, so Digby's an Old English Sheepdog who swallows a growth formula and just carries on growing. And growing. And growing. Allegedly. Can the scientist who invented the growth formula knock up something to reverse the process before the British military have to blow up Digby with big guns? Pfffffffft.

Anyone sensing a hint of *Alice's Adventures in Wonderland* here? Alice, who swallowed a potion that made her grow huge, then found one that shrank her back to normal size?

SUBSTITUTE

a shaggy dog for the little girl,
lose the White Rabbit,
the March Hare,
the Mad Hatter,
the Dormouse,
the King, Queen and Knave of Hearts,
the Cheshire Cat,
Ellie, Lacie, Tillie,
Five, Seven and Two,
the Gryphon,
two guinea pigs,
the Cook,
12 jurors,
some flamingos and hedgehogs,
the Mock Turtle,
the Caterpillar,
a puppy,
Dinah the cat,
a mouse, duck and dodo,
Mary Ann, Pat and Bill,
Old Crab and daughters,
Fish-Footman, Frog-Footman,
a pigeon and assorted other minor characters – and
you have precisely the same story!

I think you can see what I'm suggesting. That *Digby, the Biggest Dog in the World* appears to have been heavily influenced by a fictional work. That potions that make dogs grow to the size of 20 elephants do not exist. That Digby was as likely to have been the World's Biggest Dog for real – a record actually held, I seem to recall, by Bobby the Bichon Frise (though some allege that he was standing on a giraffe at the time) – as I am to have been the World's Stupidest Dog.

I realize that I'm pioneering this theory, but it is the pioneers who stick their necks out who end up in history books.

Things for Dogs to Build

6. Laboratory

This exercise is specifically for those touched by philanthropy, having read 'Ten Ways to Pass the Time' (see page 48), but also for anyone who has dipped into and been intrigued by *Beginner's Chemistry For Dogs*, which I recommend vociferously. Said tome forms the backbone of the Teach Yourself section of my library, which also includes:

- *How To Wear A Hat*
- *So You Think You're Lousy At Algebra? Think Again, Thicko!*
- *A Dog's Guide to Glass-Blowing: Volume III*
- *I've Encountered The Hair-Bear Bunch – Now How Can I Help Them?*

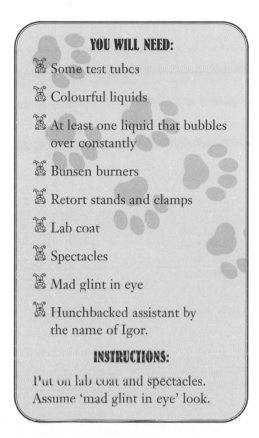

YOU WILL NEED:

- Some test tubes
- Colourful liquids
- At least one liquid that bubbles over constantly
- Bunsen burners
- Retort stands and clamps
- Lab coat
- Spectacles
- Mad glint in eye
- Hunchbacked assistant by the name of Igor.

INSTRUCTIONS:

Put on lab coat and spectacles. Assume 'mad glint in eye' look.

You are now ready to assemble your laboratory. It doesn't really matter how you do this, as long as anyone visiting the place can clearly see your liquid that constantly bubbles over.

Now, begin experimenting!

(I'm afraid I can't offer any tips on that cancer cure. Ask Igor. There's a chance his instructions might lead you to create Frankenhound during an electrical storm. If that happens, cackle like a lunatic and cry, 'I've done it! I have brought the dead back to life!' Or failing that, 'Woof!')

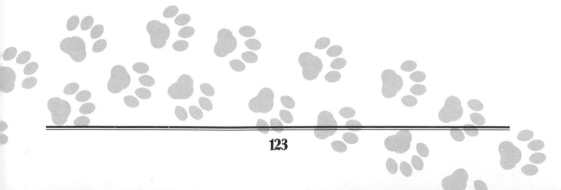

Some Things a Dog Might Eat

- Dog food
- Biscuits
- Offal
- Pies
- Gravy
- Grass
- Grasshoppers
- Shoes
- Electrical Wires
- Children's toys
- Tennis balls
- A pair of trousers

That stuff in the bottom of that tin you found in the garage

School homework

Library books

DVD players

Drain cleaner

Bones

An inner-tube

A bitter-tasting lump of meat-looking stuff already rejected by four different goats

Cats

Cat food

Cat litter

Used tissues

Nappies out of the garbage

Bird droppings

Assorted stools

Occasional tables

Pigs' ears

Wax

A candle

Plastic bags

Figs

Dates

The 15th of January

Brillo pads

Fluff and string

Bras

Socks

Men's underpants

Anything else on the floor

The floor

Mothballs

Golf balls

Meat balls

More pies

Everything else.

Games Dogs Can Play

6. Hide and Seek

We don't just love to find things we've buried in the ground. The game's a lot easier if you're not constantly having to paw at the earth, and the humans have a name for it: it's called Hide and Seek. One of you hides, the other seeks! Simple! But I have a variation on the theme which I think you're going to enjoy.

RULES:

1. Make sure you play this game outside – you'll see why shortly – ideally close to your house. The garden is perfect.

2. Let your human companion know you want to play the game. This can take a while, as they're pretty thick. Try running away from them, hiding behind something and poking your head out expectantly every few seconds. If that fails, walk in a circle around the yard holding a placard that reads: 'I WANT TO PLAY HIDE AND SEEK!'

3. Now. The cunning part. Wait until it's your human's turn to hide. Pretend to count to 100, but the moment they're out of sight, dash inside, open the treat cupboard and scoff the lot as quickly as possible.

4. If you can actually move after that, consider trying to find your human. (Have a heart.) Mind you, it's far easier to wait until they get bored and come to you.

How to... Pretend You're French

You never know when this might come in handy. Admittedly neither do I. But it's best to prepare for any eventuality.

> 1. Carry a baguette.
>
> 2. I can't think of anything else, but I reckon that should do it.
>
> 3. No, berets are a cliché.
>
> 4. Yes, so are strings of garlic.

If Pigs Might Fly, Might Dogs Too?

'**P**igs might fly,' goes the popular human saying. And if that's possible, then why not dogs too? It's a lovely thought, isn't it? Bet you can picture yourself swooping low over the countryside, spotting postmen to hassle or dogs of the opposite sex to flirt with, a gift-wrapped bone in your teeth and your flying collar turned up…

When humans picture squadrons of living bacon flying overhead above them it's an ironic thing.

WELL STOP PICTURING IT NOW, YOU GULLIBLE MUTT. IT AIN'T HAPPENING.

The clue's in the 'might'. Pigs

MIGHT

fly. And so

MIGHT

big boulders, trees the size of Liechtenstein and duck-billed platypuses.

BUT THEY DON'T!

Not actually feasible

MAN: 'You'll grow to love me one day.'

WOMAN: 'Yes. And pigs might fly.'

She isn't suddenly wondering about the aerodynamics of the average Mr Pig, debating whether his squiggly tail might act as a useful aileron. In her delirium at being chatted up by a man with one eye lower than the other, she isn't planning to turn the world of aviation on its head by launching pigs towards Jamaica with young sun-seekers on their backs. She hasn't put a finger to her lips, raised her eyes towards heaven and mused, 'I wonder what the lift-to-drag ratio of young Porky here is?'

No. SHE'S PUTTING HIM DOWN.

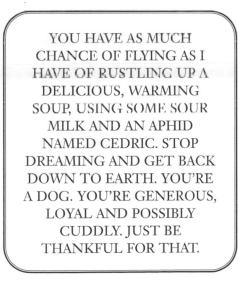

YOU HAVE AS MUCH CHANCE OF FLYING AS I HAVE OF RUSTLING UP A DELICIOUS, WARMING SOUP, USING SOME SOUR MILK AND AN APHID NAMED CEDRIC. STOP DREAMING AND GET BACK DOWN TO EARTH. YOU'RE A DOG. YOU'RE GENEROUS, LOYAL AND POSSIBLY CUDDLY. JUST BE THANKFUL FOR THAT.

Every Dog Has His Day (Or Does He?)

A phrase in common parlance, it means that every single dog, no matter how long (or short) he lives, will achieve something great once. At least it could mean that, but it doesn't actually, since it was written by humans. What it actually means is this: that every human has his moment in the limelight (and sod the dogs).

Consider these tales of canine friends I have known.

GALAXY

Galaxy used to gaze at the moon every night from the window of his lounge, as it scattered its silvery hue upon him and made him feel magical. And he would dream, every night, of setting foot on that same moon, to leap, gravity-light, as if he were a floaty puppy.

He never made it.

It never happened.

FLOSSIE

Flossie coveted the sleek-coated Afghan Hound across the road. And he fancied her, she could tell, because when they looked out of the window at each other he licked his lips. Usually, they were walked at different times, so never had the chance to meet... until one day.

That marvellous day, Flossie's human companion stubbed his toe on the way out of the house and was delayed while bandaging it. The sun was shining, her heart was racing, the wide open spaces were beckoning. When finally he went to leave, the front door of the house opposite was opening too. And there was her dynamic Afghan Hound! She leapt towards him, heart soaring...

...only to see the human opposite hurriedly bundle the Afghan back indoors with a cry of, 'My Afghan's pedigree – I'm not having him anywhere near your mangy old loser!'

The next day a removals van appeared and the Afghan and his human companions moved to Siberia.

SPOT

Plain old Spot by day, by night – or rather 'by the time he was entered into Crufts', but that doesn't scan particularly neatly – he became Emperor Caesar the Most Agile. And indeed Spot was recognized as the most agile dog of his generation. Day after day, he would practise an obstacle course in his garden, in his bid to win the prestigious agility competition at Crufts. Practise, practise, practise, until the fateful day arrived.

But Spot/Emperor Caesar the Most Agile was so nervous that he developed constipation, which only disappeared during his first round, when he stepped on to the seesaw. Unable to contain himself, he pooped at one end and leapt in haste on to the other, catapulting his poop up, up, up, then down, down, down, to land in the lap of the chief judge, one Lady Wilhelmina Smythe, who leapt up shrieking, brushing furiously at her skirt with a hankie.

He didn't win the competition that year (obviously) and was too embarrassed ever to show his face at Crufts again.

STEVE

Steve always hated the name Steve and could never get over it.

Uses of the Word 'Dog'

I t's strange how many uses of the word 'dog' there are in the English language. When all is said and done, this just shows what important animals we are. Here are some examples:

1. A DOG

As a noun. The most obvious and noblest usage. A dog. A faithful, generous and lovely creature of the canine persuasion.

2. TO DOG

As a verb. To dog someone means to pester them unremittingly, to 'hound' them. Which is strange because I am a 'dog' (even a 'hound', if you prefer), yet I have never 'dogged' anyone, let alone their footsteps. This can't be right.

3. DOGGED

As an adverb. (Or should that be 'adjective'? It's all rather confusing, the English language.) If one has 'dogged' determination, it means that one is being egged on by a series of dogs. I think.

4. DOGGING

Oh dear, my printer's just run out of in

Learn to Recognize the World's Scariest Words

T he two worst words in the world are 'neutering' and 'spaying'. They are Not Good. At All. No No. Let me explain. Neutering – and I should know, I've had it done – involves (you may wish to tense some groin muscles while wincing) removing a dog's testicles. Humans maintain there are good reasons for it. I would suggest that if I tried to explain to a male human the 'good reasons' for removing his testicles, he would swiftly be inclined to demur. Now that's hypocrisy. You don't see male humans taking their dog to the vet for neutering, saying to the vet – in the interests of solidarity – 'Do me first'. It doesn't happen.

> TAKE IT FROM ME: A DOG WITHOUT HIS BALLS IS LIKE A BASEBALL
> PLAYER WITHOUT HIS BALL. WAVING A BIG STICK AT THIN AIR.

The same goes for 'spaying', which happens to female dogs. I have no idea what the surgical procedure involves – and I have no wish to know – but take it from me, it's the female equivalent of neutering, so it ain't good.

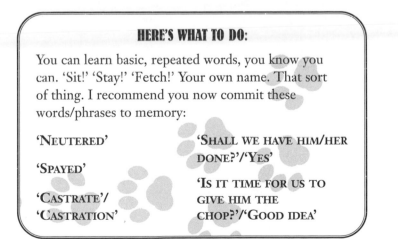

HERE'S WHAT TO DO:

You can learn basic, repeated words, you know you can. 'Sit!' 'Stay!' 'Fetch!' Your own name. That sort of thing. I recommend you now commit these words/phrases to memory:

'NEUTERED'

'SPAYED'

'CASTRATE'/
'CASTRATION'

'SHALL WE HAVE HIM/HER
DONE?'/'YES'

'IS IT TIME FOR US TO
GIVE HIM THE
CHOP?'/'GOOD IDEA'

If you hear any of these being bandied about by your human companions, you have but one option. RUN! When exhaustion compels you to stop, take a breather. Then run some more.

I've heard there's a community of dogs in France, all happily possessing full genitalia, who have gathered there to seek sanctuary. Head there if you can – provided you're fond of puppies and they'll let you in.

Things for Dogs to Build

7. Plate Tipper

This one's a cracker. I've used it successfully so many times that my human companions have taken to dining behind locked doors. With my patented Plate Tipper, there's no more staring patiently at their food as they eat – now you can make the food come to you!

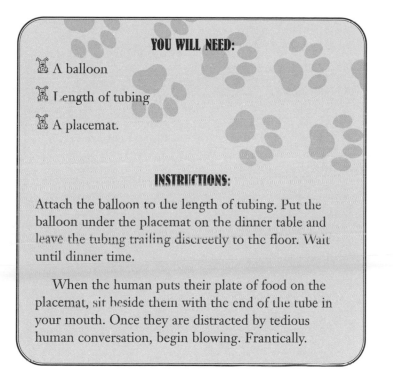

YOU WILL NEED:

🐾 A balloon

🐾 Length of tubing

🐾 A placemat.

INSTRUCTIONS:

Attach the balloon to the length of tubing. Put the balloon under the placemat on the dinner table and leave the tubing trailing discreetly to the floor. Wait until dinner time.

When the human puts their plate of food on the placemat, sit beside them with the end of the tube in your mouth. Once they are distracted by tedious human conversation, begin blowing. Frantically.

HERE'S WHAT HAPPENS:

As the balloon inflates, it tips the plate of food. Until eventually the food slides off the plate – with you underneath it, gob open, ready to catch the lot!

Famous Dogs in History

6. Rin-Tin-Tin

Celebrated German Shepherd of radio and screen, from the 1920s and 1930s. What the unsuspecting public did not realize was that Rin-Tin-Tin actually was a German shepherd, named Hans Krüger, who one day lost all his sheep in dense fog and so developed a sideline in doing quite good dog impressions.

This deceit was easy enough to perpetuate on radio, with Hans barking his way through a series of exciting dog-based adventures, starting with *Rin-Tin-Tin The Wonder Dog (1928)*. Here are two sample scenes:

> **BILLY:** Save me from this masked armed man, Rin-Tin-Tin!
>
> **RIN-TIN-TIN/HANS:** Wuff! Wuff! Grrrrrr!
>
> **MASKED ARMED MAN:** That pesky dog's too strong for me. I give up!
>
> **BILLY:** Gee, thanks, Rin-Tin-Tin, you're swell!

BILLY: Leap into that burning building, Rin-Tin-Tin, grab the crying baby, then throw yourself and the kid into the river and swim to safety, using your tail as a makeshift propeller!

RIN-TIN-TIN/HANS: Wuff! Wuff! Wuff!

SOUND EFFECTS: CRYING, LESS CRYING, THEN SPLASHING.

BILLY [AFTER A BIT]: Nice work, Rin-Tin-Tin!

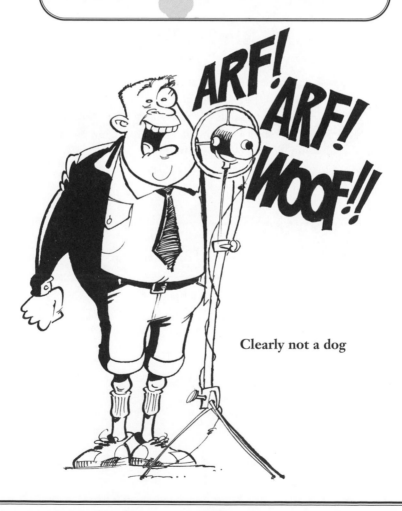

Clearly not a dog

As you can see, the radio audience was able to fill in the action using their imagination. Everyone loved Rin-Tin-Tin (who was actually a shepherd named Hans, remember). Then some bright spark invented cinema.

Obviously, people were going to spot that Hans, who was six foot tall, wore a monocle and walked with a limp, was not really a dog. Drastic action was called for, so the producers shot Hans and buried him in some woods.

Next they drafted in a proper German Shepherd dog, named Tony. Sadly, Tony took to leaping into burning buildings like a duck to lava to rescue babies. His first motion picture, *Rin-Tin-Tin Saves Manhattan* (1934), became a major flop since the only stunt that Tony was prepared to perform was eating Slush Puppies until he developed an ice-cream headache.

For all other action sequences, the producers resorted to desperate measures. As the most celebrated movie reviewer of the time, Hiram P Testaburger, put it: 'We early cinema-goers may not be sophisticated. Neither are we so stupid that we cannot spot that – besides in the scene where Rin-Tin-Tin consumes too much icy drink – our canine hero is actually a man in a dog suit.'

Drastic action was again called for, so the producers shot Tony and buried him next to Hans.

THEN ONE OF THE PRODUCERS
HAD A BRIGHT IDEA:

'Sod the dog thing,'

HE SUGGESTED.

'Let's drop the Rin bit, just call
him Tin-Tin, and relaunch him
as a lanky Belgian with a
stupid quiff.'

Tintin was born and the rest is history.

Why Small Dogs Think They're Hard

They have a phrase for this in human terminology. They call it Small Man Syndrome (or Tom Cruise, for short). It's when a man isn't very tall, so he tries to act bigger to compensate for this, perhaps by hiding stilts under his trousers, or by always standing on a box, or by only ever being spotted in the middle of a group of children (this is why most male teachers are short).

In small dogs, it manifests itself in different ways. I knew one Dachshund who only ever rode around on a horse. But generally Small Dog Syndrome makes them aggressive little blighters – overcompensating for their silly stature – always itching for a fight with their high-pitched 'Yap! Yap! Yap!'. We've all seen it, in the local park: a Jack Russell with all the machismo of an old lady knitting baby booties launching itself at a passing Doberman.

When you're a good-sized dog like myself, such behaviour is hardly intimidating. (I once growled back at a Shih Tzu so ferociously that it lived up to its name and we all had to walk around in wellingtons afterwards.) But it can be extremely annoying.

So here are some ways to deal with irritating small dogs bedevilled by Small Dog Syndrome:

> **1.** Try the growling method (as above) – first making sure that you can put your paws on some wellingtons at short notice.
>
> **2.** Tell them that you know their parents, and if they carry on like that you'll make sure they get a jolly good spanking when they get home.
>
> **3.** Tie them to a helium balloon. 'See how you like yapping at the birds, Titch!'

4. Suggest to them that you have seen bigger, and more terrifying gerbils. If this only infuriates them further, resort to 1.

5. Pretend to search the area wearing a 'You're so teeny I can't even see you' T-shirt. Again, this may require resorting to 1.

6. Taunt them with some platform shoes you bought earlier, but which they can't have.

7. Stuff them into a walnut shell, tape it shut and sell them as Mexican jumping beans.

(If these methods sound belittling to small dogs, fear not: they can't get much littler.)

How To... Learn to Love Yourself

Dogs spend so much time being lovely to everyone else, worrying about whether others love them. That's fine, that's what we do – but you should also find the space for a little Me Time. Go on, you deserve it. Patchouli oil dabbed on to a handkerchief and placed under the left front paw works well with this.

1. Stand in front of a mirror.

2. Open your mouth.

3. Breathe in deeply, exhale slowly.

4. Begin meditation by going 'Ommmmm' (or, failing that, 'Wooooooooooooof').

5. STOP worrying whether your owners love you! Of course they do!

6. YES, I promise!

7. I just know.

8. No, you don't need to go and check.

9. GET BACK HERE!

10. I don't believe you.

11. But you've only just had dinner.

12. You're not going to check whether you left anything in your dog bowl, you're sneaking off to toady to your owner!

13. I just know.

14. Look, this is about Learning to Love Yourself and not needing constant reassurance.

15. Yes, I'm sure they love you.

16. Yes, I'm sure.

17. Call it intuition.

18. OK, now clear your mind.

19. YES, I'M SURE!

20. NO, THAT WASN'T HER CALLING YOU JUST THEN!

21. If I hear her calling, yes, I will let you know. Now, can we concentrate? Good.

22. Clear your mind.

23. NO, SHE DIDN'T LEAVE THE KITCHEN DOOR OPEN!

24. YES, SHE HAS HER SLIPPERS!

25. NO, YOU DIDN'T HEAR
    SOMEONE PROWLING
    AROUND IN THE LOFT!

26. AAAAAGH!

27. YES, I BLOODY DO HATE
    YOU. YOU'RE INSECURE,
    INSUFFERABLE...

28. Wait! Come back! Please! I
    didn't mean it.

29. [Whistles to self.]

30. So then.

Games Dogs Can Play

7. Tug of War

Traditionally, the game as played between dog and human involves the dog holding one end of something (a stick, say), the human holding the other, and the both of them tugging. The one who lets go of the object first loses, often resulting in them flying backwards with considerable momentum. All fine and dandy. Except...

I've been looking into this Tug of War business and it seems, when the game is played only by humans, that *teams* are usually employed, with each tugging on one end of a rope. These teams can employ four, five, six – any number of humans.

It seems that we dogs have been cheated.

So next time you're after a game of Tug of War with your human companion, *prepare first*. Contact all your mates. Give them a time and a place and get them to hide around a corner.

When the game is about to begin, a quick bark as a signal and out they pour – and suddenly you're taking on a human using the proper rules.

That should do it.

8. Zoot Suit

YOU WILL NEED:

🐾 A zoot

🐾 A suit (I've played cards, so there's no fooling me on this one – pick any one from diamonds, spades, hearts or clubs. I'll go spades, since diamonds are too expensive, hearts are too gross and clubs are way too violent. So the list actually runs…)

YOU WILL NEED:

🐾 A zoot

🐾 Some spades (three should suffice, let's not get too greedy – dig it?!)

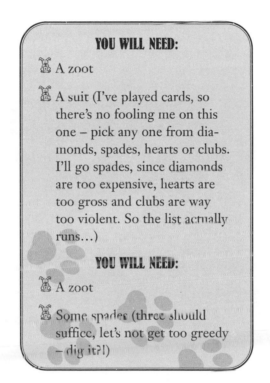

INSTRUCTIONS:

Admittedly, I'm not sure what a zoot is either, but I'm prepared to stick my neck out, using my years of wisdom and knowledge of the street. I know you wear this zoot thing, and I know it's cool, so I reckon a zoot looks pretty much like this:

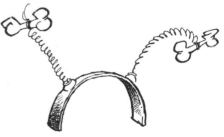

Now, as I said before, I'm not entirely sure what a zoot suit is, but I've heard that all the cool cats – and dogs, natch – wear one. So I'm going to wing it, and I'd be surprised if I got it wrong.

All you gotta do now is put it all together:

Lookin' cool in ma zoot suit!

Now tell me I'm wrong! Tell me that's not the hippest lookin' zoot suit you ever did see! Cos if that ain't, I'm a monkey's uncle!

ME   MY NEPHEW

Things for Dogs to Build

ICE-CREAM CONE

MOON

KITCHEN FOIL

DUSTBINS

Advanced: Space Rocket

If you've successfully built the previously outlined projects in this book, you might like to attempt my Advanced option. Think about it: have you ever wished you could go into space, just like Laika? (Any dog answering that with a 'Yes' should probably avoid reading 'Famous Dogs in History 2: Laika' on page 30.)

Here's how!

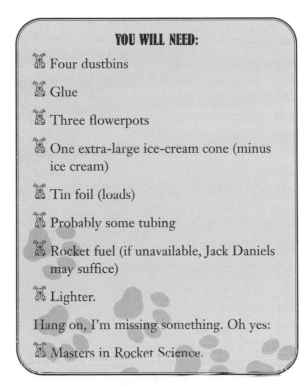

YOU WILL NEED:

🐾 Four dustbins

🐾 Glue

🐾 Three flowerpots

🐾 One extra-large ice-cream cone (minus ice cream)

🐾 Tin foil (loads)

🐾 Probably some tubing

🐾 Rocket fuel (if unavailable, Jack Daniels may suffice)

🐾 Lighter.

Hang on, I'm missing something. Oh yes:

🐾 Masters in Rocket Science.

I did say it was the Advanced option!

INSTRUCTIONS:

1. Glue the dustbins on top of each other.

2. Glue the flowerpots to the bottom of the lowest dustbin, as boosters.

3. Glue the ice-cream cone on top.

4. Cover in tin foil. (Looks space-age!)

5. Glue tubing somewhere. (Ditto.)

6. Pour in rocket fuel.

You are ready to take to the skies!

Hmm, best of luck with that. You might want to warn the neighbours.

Some Things Dogs Might Say (If They Could Talk Human)

It's very easy for humans to say talk is cheap, but the fact of the matter is that 'woof!' often doesn't cover it. Here are some examples:

HUMAN:
'That lady-dog across the road sure seems to like you!'

ME: 'Woof!'

(actually, that's one instance where it *does* work)

HUMAN:
'Hey, boy, would you like some treats?'

ME: 'Woof!'

HUMAN: 'Who wants to go for a walk on the beach?'

ME: 'Woof!'

HUMAN:
'Who wants to eat beetles for a living?'

ME: 'Woof!'

HUMAN:
'You've left a turd in the sink!'

ME: 'Woof!'

HUMAN:
'Right, first one to go "Woof!" has to wear a dress!'

ME:
[THOUGH DESPERATELY TRYING TO CHOKE IT BACK]: 'Woof!'

I hope you get my drift. So here are some things dogs might like to say, if only they could talk human:

UNACCUSTOMED AS I AM TO PUBLIC SPEAKING

VOTES FOR DOGS

'Can I have some treats, please?'

'Yes, more treats!'

'Of course I'm not full yet!'

'You want it so badly, you fetch it.'

'Please would you tell that small child to stop picking up my ear and peering into the hole?'

'Look. Naff. off.'

'That lady over there's up for it. Let go of the lead. Let go of the lead!'

'You wouldn't understand.'

'Yes, more treats!'

'Can I have your leftovers?'

'I don't care if I am in the middle of the floor. I'm resting.'

'Well, I'm not cleaning it up!'

'You be Shaggy, I'll be Scooby.'

'I'm a bit scared of Michael Jackson.'

Some Things Dogs Might Do
(If They Had Opposable Thumbs)

our legs good, two legs bad, wrote George Orwell, but he
made no mention of opposable thumbs. Here are examples of
how we could do with them:

> HUMAN:
> 'We're all going to climb this rope-ladder to reach the
> tree house in the branches, then we're all going to
> have a great time!'
>
> ME:
> (Looks on enviously while feeling left out)
>
>
> HUMAN:
> 'I'm going to breakdance and all my friends are going
> to think I'm really cool and rhythmic!'
>
> ME:
> (Shuffles paws distractedly while feeling frustrated)
>
>
> HUMAN:
> 'I'm going to loft a thumb in the manner of Paul
> McCartney – being the international gesture that
> something is "OK".'
>
> ME:
> (Stares at paw moodily while hating self)

> 🧍 HUMAN:
> 'I'm going to simply pick up something – wait for it...
> Without using my teeth!'
>
> 🐰 ME:
> (Growls, bares teeth; launches self at human, rips
> bloody head off)

I hope you get my drift. So here are some things dogs might like to do, if only they had opposable thumbs:

> 🐰 Drink from a cup/mug (so much less degrading)
>
> 🐰 Eat with a knife and fork (ditto)
>
> 🐰 Ah, what the hell – use chop-sticks
>
> 🐰 Beckon ladies over
>
> 🐰 Catch the bloody stick and throw it in a hedge
>
> 🐰 Ditto the ball
>
> 🐰 Play computer games
>
> 🐰 Do that Paul McCartney thumb thing
>
> 🐰 Play the bass guitar

🐰 Pan for gold.

🐰 Greet VIPs with a handshake

🐰 Pinch ladies' bottoms

🐰 Write to humans, just to show off

🐰 Make paper-planes and fly them

🐰 Breakdance (maybe not).

Another one springs to mind, but I think I'll leave it there.

Byyyeee!

I hope you've enjoyed my pearls of wisdom, my gifts from the doggy's mouth, my sweet knowledge nectar. If you didn't quite get some of my ideas, maybe you should read it again, cos it all made perfect sense to me.

I leave you with this simple set of rules. Live by these and you will be happy. Here they are:

- **P**lay dumb (as if you would be!)
- **E**at lots
- **E**at more
- **F**etch things (until you get old like me, then consult my book)
- **R**un around a bit
- **E**at more than that
- **E**njoy yourself!
- **L**ove everyone
- **Y**earn for treats.

I'd give it an acronym to help you remember it, but I just can't think of one.

Be seein' ya!
JASON X